HERE I AM:
Lessons Learned

A GUIDE TO A NEW AND FULLER LIFE

Dr. Irene Estay

BALBOA.
PRESS

A DIVISION OF HAY HOUSE

Balboa Press books may be ordered through booksellers or by contacting:

Balboa Press
A Division of Hay House
1663 Liberty Drive
Bloomington, IN 47403
www.balboapress.com
1-(877) 407-4847

Printed in the United States of America.

ISBN: 978-1-4525-8186-6 (sc)
ISBN: 978-1-4525-8188-0 (hc)
ISBN: 978-1-4525-8187-3 (e)

Library of Congress Control Number: 2013916309

Balboa Press rev. date: 09/25/2013

TABLE OF CONTENTS

ACKNOWLEDGEMENTS

Not different from others, my life journey has not been an easy one. And, from encounters with many individuals through my life to this day, I have learned many lessons – lessons on compassion, resiliency, courage and forgiveness.

From the lessons that gave me the most pain, but also the most insights, I learned to let go and move on. My most difficult experiences have allowed me to 'connect' with those that, having similar difficult experiences, are also learning to let go and move on.

Once I discovered my purpose in life, my Lessons Learned helped me to transmit those lessons to others. As for me, I have been able to discard both resentments and the 'aches' that I had been carrying for years. Through sharing my experiences, having placed them in the context of my empowerment seminars, I love the end result – participants also are able to 'let go' and move forward in their lives.

First of all, I must recognize and thank the 'angels' in my life. They came dressed in many garments and took on several roles in teaching me the lessons that now guide my life and teaching. Among the long list of 'angels', I include my late mother; my brother and sister; the Floridenas of my life; my spouse (my life companion of, now, 43 years); my two sons, Daniel and Andre; and the latest members of our family, my daughters-in-law, Melissa and Allison, and my two beautiful grandsons, Drayden and Jacob.

In my journey, there have been and are other individuals and groups that have and do support me, trusting in my endeavors. They have been fully behind my Empowerment Seminars, supporting the seminars in many ways, including financial. I particularly note my fellow *Lions* members from the *Lions Club of Calgary*, who have assisted me over the years with yearly donations to the Seminars that are now held in several languages.

Calgary Family Services for their unconditional support to the Empowerment Seminars and also in encouraging any grow that we have attempted over the years with new audiences and in different languages.

I also recognize and thank *Prospect Human Services*, an organization that supports vulnerable individuals. This organization allows me to enter into their culture, helping their clients reach their potential. Over time, I have been fortunate to, through the Lessons Learned content, able to inspire many of their employees to become *Floridenas* for individuals that need support in their life journeys.

Special appreciation goes to Graham Lane, who edited this book giving form and structure to what initially was a rough manuscript. His wisdom and experience, drawn in part from a late career as a judge, helped focus the message to allow it to be more easily received by individuals striving to enhance their lives one step at a time.

And, finally, a special thanks to the two individuals who have been with me from the start of my own growth path, Luis and Pat. My life partner, Luis, is the love of my life as well as my 'rock'. My sister Pat shares the bonds of sisterhood with me, being as well a traveler on a similar path. We are also friends, confidents and colleagues (since 2008, when she took over managing the seminars, she has relentlessly advanced the progress of them).

I have been fortunate to find many travelers willing to lend me a hand and for that I am grateful and also committed to help others in their journey when crossing pass or when needing an extra hand.

CHAPTER 1

INTRODUCTION

Through this book, I hope to help those having difficulty with their life.

I am a practicing psychologist that has, now for fourteen years, put on seminars with that objective. The seminars empower participants to realize their dreams and potential, while better enjoying their lives through making changes. Making changes to one's outlook on and attitudes to life, changes that affect every dimension of one's life, is not easy. Yet, it is necessary if one wants to discover and live the happier life they want and are best suited for.

Before anyone can make changes in their life, they have to understand where they came from. Memories of past experiences, both happy and unpleasant, need to be retrieved from our memory banks (our brains). Once retrieved, those memories can be assessed and reassessed, and we can decide, yes decide, to take their power away if they are interfering with our present.

Memories of past events, whether conscious or absent in our conscience, drive our reactions to present events, and either facilitate or restrict our options and actions.

In this book, I begin by reviewing my own early life. I describe the conditions and events that affected my childhood, siblings and other family members. I speculate on the events that eventually led me to who I am, what I have done, and what I do now. By being open about my own life, I hope to engender your trust, so as to better allow you to consider my specific recommendations for your gaining and maintaining a better, happier and more purposeful, life.

And, after reviewing my experiences (reclaiming memories, re-wiring my brain for success, and obtaining my academic qualifications), I report on how my empowerment seminars came about. After relating the case histories of some of the past participants in the seminars, I then provide, through twenty one assignments, including a self-agreement, a guide for those willing and determined to undertake self-help 'work' towards changing their lives for the better.

Even if, through undertaking the assignments, you only come to have a better understanding of your feelings and the obstacles that you either have had or are now encountering, I suspect you will 'change', and will begin to live a happier, more fulsome and purposeful life. And, beyond that, through the 'assignments' I provide the means to free yourself of emotional burdens that may have been holding you back from the fulsome and enjoyable life that you should and could have—a life that will not only enhance your own happiness and purpose in life, but also enhance the lives of those around you, particularly those you care most about.

The idea for this book arose out of my empowerment seminars. My friends and associates have helped me design and hold the seminars on a regular basis. Over the years, an innumerable number of people have attended and been helped.

By your reading of the obstacles that I have encountered and how I managed to overcome them, and by your working your way through the 'assignments', my hope for you is that you too will rewire your brain and then enjoy your life journey since we only do it once (as far as we can remember!). So make every day count and when you get to the end of the journey you can sigh with relief that you did have a fulfilling life!

CHAPTER 2

HERE I AM, LESSONS LEARNED

After all the time that has come and gone in my life, and thinking as to what I can offer others from what I have learned (from the experiences of my own life's journey), I have come to the realization that the simple process of living, which involves innumerable challenges and obstacles requiring constant changes, serves as a common denominator for everyone.

This allows the possibility that by my recounting my experiences and reflections, I can act as a catalyst to assist others as they complete their own life's journey.

I am in front of my computer, letting my fingers do the talking. I have had a life of learning, one full of changes and surprises. I have almost experienced too many 'twists and turns' during my life's journey to-date to recall. And, often at the time the "twists and turns" occurred, I was unable to explain how or why they had come about. Yet, now, some of those 'twists and turns' make sense, looking at the events from the vantage point of the 'here and now'.

As to some other events, I have yet to make sense of them. For them, I must accept that this is not the time for me to know the 'why' of those 'happenings'. I expect everything will be revealed to me in time, but just not now.

When I look back in my life, I realize that in every circumstance I was never alone. Either something or someone was guiding me, even during the hardest of times. This was especially true when I was young, then very much feeling alone and without great support. Now, years later, with the advantage that comes with experience and much reflection, I realize that I was never really, absolutely, alone.

Somehow, even in the worst of times, the person or persons I needed showed up, and at the right time to make a difference. Fortunately, I have always been a good listener, and I have applied the learning I was fortunate to receive at every step of my journey.

Early Years

My first memory I recall has me standing on my father's feet, dancing to loud music. Was that the day my mind truly opened to this world? I remember going around and around and feeling dizzy, in awe, dancing, moving easily with the rythm.

My father was a real character. He loved life and was always doing fun things with us, his family, I am sure my brother has his own happy memories of those much too brief time with our father. But, as my sister was a baby when my father died, unfortunately, she doesn't have those memories of him.

If I close my eyes and focus on my childhood memories, I go back to the house we lived in. Though I would then have been only two or three years old. I remember the big hallways, heavy doors and huge furniture (furniture so big that I couldn't climb into bed, and had to get a stool). Everything in our house now seems to have been big and heavy, No surprise, given my then-age. The sink faucets were out of reach for me, I couldn't get a sip of water on my own. As for the cabinets, I was unable to fit my hand around the handle to open them; my hand was much too small.

I remember lining up for candy. The candy ceremony happened when dad came home from work, and he was the only one with a key for the cabinet that contained the treasured loot. We knew when he was coming home. "Biddu", our shaggy black and grey dog, would run around and around the house seconds before dad opened the door and loudly announced his return.

Our routine was always the same. Right after father showed up, Biddu would rush to be first in line for the candy. We had no chance to out-race Biddu. I remember the hallways 'doubling' in size every time I ran to the cabinet, always losing the race to Biddu. Nobody, not even my brother who was (and still is) bigger and faster than me, and able to open the cabinet doors with only one of his hands, could beat Biddu.

By the time I got to the cabinet, Biddu had already got his treat. If I tried to get ahead of Biddu, he would peel back his teeth as if he saying "don't you dare take my spot". Yet, he never bit any of us, though for me his sneer was enough to wet my cheeks with tears. In the end, I had to accept being either second or third in line, my placement depending on how generous my brother was that day (my baby sister was not part of the race).

I also remember being carried on my father's shoulders as we came home on Sunday evenings after either having had a full day of fun at the park or from visiting our grandparents. I was so tired I could no longer walk and would fall asleep on the bus. When it was time to walk the rest of the way home, I would cry and dad would place me on his shoulders.

Great memories! Yet, I remember that my crying was required. If I didn't cry, I had to walk (like a "big girl") the three blocks from the bus stop to our house.

Funny thing, now looking back, while my baby sister must have been there she is not anywhere to be found in my earliest memories. Perhaps I had inadvertently chosen to ignore her, as she was not part of the 'candy line-up'. As well, she was too small to be carried on my father's shoulders.

Another possibility comes to mind. It is possible that I have difficulty recalling her in those early scenes of my childhood bliss because she was my 'competition' from the day she was born until my maturity. Likely, in the walks to and from the bus, she was just bundled up and put in a stroller. She definitely was in my blind spot, then, leaving Biddu and my older brother in the recalled scenes of my very early life.

The strongest of my early memories is of an event that led to the first 'major turn' in my life. It is of a day when I stood on a kitchen stool so I could reach the sink. I wanted to wash my hands before my dad got home and the candy ceremony took place. And, that day, I was excited to show him my new school uniform. In a few months, I would start school and a neighbour had just brought me my uniform so I could try it on. (She had hand-sewed the uniform for me, it must have taken her some time to do!)

From my stand on the stool, I saw a group of people bringing a sobbing woman into our house. Who was she? Why is she crying? Why are so many other people coming into our house? Why is nobody paying any attention to me? Where is my dad? I want dad right now!

Tragedy

With time, I have been able to better piece my memories together, allowing me to realize what was actually happening and why. The sobbing woman was my mother. My father had died that day in a hospital emergency room, and nobody knew why. To this day, I am still unaware of the exact cause of his early departure from our lives.

As usual, over the weekend we had visited my grandparents. This time, my dad fell ill and my mom took him to the hospital's emergency clinic. My aunt brought me home and stayed with me overnight. My brother was taken to another aunt's home. I don't recall where my baby sister went, probably she was left with our grandparents

My mother was only 29 when her husband died. Today, sixty-four years later, I still don't know the medical cause for why my father left us so suddenly. In those days, nobody told you anything. If somebody died, too bad: ". . . your husband is dead, go home" was the approach.

So, no one bothered to explain to us what had happened to him, even though providing the reason for his death would have only taken an extra minute or so, and would have helped our family make some sense of the cause of our new reality.

That day my life changed, dramatically and forever.

As I recall that moment now, I had a typical childhood reaction, I feared I was the cause, maybe I did something very wrong and my dad decided to leave. No more running around, riding on his shoulders or candy line-ups. And to top it all off, Biddu died two days after my father passed away.

I always wonder what my life would have been if my father hadn't left us so early and so suddenly. Or, what would be my life if I was born into a totally different family, or if my mother had been more skillful in raising three young children, including a baby, on her own. What I do know is that my life took a different path that day, leading to who I am today.

When my dad died, I was three or four. I know that because I was going to start school, children normally began some sort of schooling at or about the age of four in Chile.

I became very excited that day, when my mom was brought into the house, sobbing. One of the women helping my mother told me that my father had died. I cannot recall my feelings, only my looking around not knowing what to think or what to feel. Likely, I was too little to even understand the meaning of death.

I was very confused and did not know what to do, so I stood on that stool for a long time. While I was getting tired, I didn't know what I would do if I got off the stool. I did realize that my uniform was getting wrinkled and wet, and I may have known that I shouldn't keep it on for the whole day.

Another thought I recall is that I couldn't wait to tell my brother that our father had died. I knew he was at our aunt's home, but I wanted to be the first to tell him. Soon after, my aunt brought him home and I ran to tell him the news. When he began to cry, I couldn't understand why.

At that age, I lacked the concepts of loss, sadness, death, even pain. Does this seem strange to you? It does for me, even now.

I had been a three or four year old happy little girl waiting for her dad to come and see her in her new uniform, a uniform that by that time was dirty and wrinkled. I kept it on, still thinking I would show it to dad, and nobody bothered to take it off. Not that day, nor the following day. I don't think my brother or me put on our pajamas that night, or for the next few nights.

Funeral and Flowers

On the day of the funeral, I was happy and excited. There were many visitors (neighbours, our grandparents, uncles and aunts) at my house. I moved my little stool around so I could better see what was going on. I looked to see who was there and what was happening. I carried my stool into the kitchen, then to the bathroom. There, I washed my hands and face by myself. And, then, with my stool, I went to the living room, which had flowers all over and around my father's coffin.

I remember standing on my stool beside my father's coffin and thinking: "What are you doing in there, daddy? And, why are you sleeping in the living room? Why don't you go to bed?"

I now realize that I was then oblivious to the sadness around me. I remained that happy little girl with a stool that made me taller and more visible everywhere I moved it to. Flowers, many flowers, all types of smells were all through the house, with me (with my little stool) having fun, reaching all the places I wanted to reach. Nobody was telling me not to do it.

I felt totally in control—of place, time, everything!

Connections

I have never liked flowers. Today, I can piece together memories of my father's passing and better understand why I am not too fond of flowers. Flowers don't bring me joy or happiness; they create "a blank" in my 'feeling' memory.

When my husband went into the flower business, this about 20 years ago, I thought it as a somber business. I couldn't imagine who would want to sell flowers. For me, flowers are linked to my father's funeral and the sobbing woman. Flowers signify, for me, times of sadness, loss and pain.

Yet, over the last twenty years I have discovered that people love flowers. And, that flowers are not just attached to death and sadness, but also to celebrations, birthdays, happy moments, special times, or, just because! It is good to accept that flowers can be uplifting, rather than being wanted only for the saddest moments of life.

It is only now that I can appreciate the pleasant meaning of flowers for others. But, for me, I cannot, at least on an emotional level, relate flowers to feelings of happiness, celebrations and good times. I still see flowers as being associated with confusion, loss, sadness, pain. My feeling about flowers is more apt for a four-year old, one forced to deal with the difficult and painful circumstances of that time.

So, at the age of four my life changed dramatically, but I didn't know that then. Now, I can recall the 'sobbing woman' sitting at the edge of a gigantic bed, with a baby lying right beside her. It took time until I was finally able to link that memory with my baby sister, who had disappeared until then from my memories of that time. Before, much later, and recognizing what was actually going on, the 'picture' in my head left out my baby sister. I had focused on an image of a sobbing woman, an image that had become so strong it became part of me.

Much later in my life, I finally understood the cause of the rather blank feeling that flowers bring to me. That feeling was exactly what I had felt when I was introduced to flowers at the age of four, upon my father's death.

One element of what I have learned about that time in my life (when I was four and my father had died), is the complexity of the mind. That complexity is evidenced by its ability, years later, to piece times and events together. Memories determine how one perceives events, with aspects of later events with similarities with earlier initial experiences affecting current memory. Future events become grounded in memories of the past, so the past, as we recall it, varies as time moves on.

The major event of my early years, the death of my father, triggered my later role as a strategist in life. Somehow or at least partially because of the early loss of my father, I became prematurely resourceful. In a way as I grew older, I took on the role of caregiver, both for my mom and my siblings.

As my mother struggled, she began to confide in me and my siblings about the difficulties she encountered. For our little family to survive we had to help her, and not just with housekeeping. In my childhood days, I was always helping mom. The asks of me included requests by my mother seeking solutions for family problems, helping around the house and fixing things. You grow up quickly when you are made responsible for things well before others are. It seems I was always needed to address issues, even when I did not have the experience, skills or abilities to do so.

On the other hand, my sister had an even harder time growing up. As a teenager, she developed severe allergies, eventually diagnosed as being the result of psychological trauma. As a result, she was in therapy for most of her teenage years. She needed help, lacking what we now know as 'Attachment'. She was so young when our father died, and she didn't bond with mom. The opportunity for her to bond with mom was taken from her when, after my father died, she was put in the care of our grandparents.

Following our father's sudden death, my mother was not emotionally healthy enough to provide the loving and nurturing relationship that any of us children needed, particularly my baby sister. At the time of our father's death my sister could not have the full attention of a mother. She lived with our grandparents and It was years later when she was returned to our house after living with our grandparents.

When reflecting about the past, I have always wondered what led me to create the successful strategies that enabled me to survive the bad times, while my sister suffered, and not just from allergies. I now recognize the importance to a child of forming a strong attachment to the child's mother.

Now, I realize that when my father died my sister was but a baby, a baby that couldn't be left in the care of a woman consumed with pain and depression. Our mother's state of mind did not allow my sister and her to create that most important of bonds, that between a mother and her baby.

For me, by the time my father left, I already had a strong 'wiring' of 'happy feelings in my brain', particularly when compared to my baby sister. Not only she didn't get to know our father, as I did, but she was not able to get the love and attention that is so needed by a baby, particularly from that *sobbing woman* seated at the edge of a gigantic bed.

Today, through making sense of my own life's journey, I have been able to formulate an approach towards helping others develop peace of mind. Using the plasticity of our minds, we have an innate power to change our lives for the better, by recalling and making sense of our memories. Once we can understand "what happened" and make peace with those times, we can reclaim our present.

Every time I go back into my memory bank and have an *'AHA!' moment* I become excited, and, using simple strategies, I have the prospect of being able to teach others to discover their own *AHA!* moments, to be drawn from their memories. From such memories, they can learn to rewire their minds, and 'mend' the memories that have negatively affected their lives, often causing a downward spiral in their interpretation of their life events.

CHAPTER 3

GRANDPA

When my father died, my mother had no idea how she would take care of her three small children, so we all became part of my grandparents' family. And, while my mother, my brother and I remained at home, my baby sister went to live with them while mom attempted to sort out her life.

Looking back, and in my effort to understand the dynamics of our surviving but suffering family, I realized that our grandpa was a bitter and resentful man. (My grandmother, a sweet and loving woman, was his victim through all of the years they were together.)

Grandpa didn't want the additional responsibility of taking care of a young family. Yet, all of a sudden, he was faced with the fact that our grandparents were going to have to take care of a baby, and he didn't know for how long. For Grandpa, having an addition to his family was neither a joy nor a blessing. So, my little sister had that cross to bear as well, not 'truly' wanted.

As I have noted, our grandpa had his own issues, and he could be tasteless and even mean. When I was little, I had very light red hair and a face full of freckles. Definitely, my colouring was not the typical description of a Latin-American child. My light skin, red hair and freckles caused me plenty of pain while growing up, and that pain began with Grandpa.

He created a story about me that became a regular topic of conversation at dinner time at his and Grandma's home. My mother, brother and I would eat there quite regularly since we would visit our sister regularly.

He would start his story by saying I was not part of the family, and that my freckles had been caused by flies that landed on my face while I lay in the garbage, where my original parents had thrown me. In his story, my "second set of parents", my actual mom and dad, had found me in the garbage can and took me in.

His story seemed to be funny for everyone else but me, I remember adults at the dinner table, neighbours, relatives and my mother, laughing with him as he told his story about my beginnings. For me, the nagging question was, is Grandpa's story true? If so, why didn't my real parents want me? What is wrong with me? Where is my real family? Why did my 'new parents' rescue me from the trash can? You shouldn't make up and tell fictional stories about important things, such stories can hurt and mar a child.

Yet, over time, I have learned it was and is quite common for adults to make up stories about children, with some of the stories, such as the one of me being found in the garbage, negatively affecting the child 'victim'. Made-up stories about children told by adults with the child the 'butt' of the joke can result in the child carrying the 'hurt' for a long time. At least that was the result in my case!

While such stories may (and I must say 'may') be meant as a joke, such jokes, particularly when told by a parent or a grandparent, can have great significance for the child. This is especially true when the child is missing the strong support needed by children either from loving and caring parents or, if that support is inadequate or missing (which was the case for me) by other close and loving caregivers.

A four year old child lacks the awareness and intellectual capability needed to be able to say to a joking adult, "Grandpa, if you repeatedly tell your made-up story about me, it is going to not only negatively affect the way I see myself but decrease the value I place on myself, and for a very long time".

What I learned from my grandpa's story about me is that, for a child, adults are assumed to be telling the truth all the time, regardless of the circumstances. Children are cognitively unable to understand when a story is a fantasy, so any story, however outrageously wrong, coming from a significant adult, will be retained by the child as 'the truth'.

Something so simple and, apparently, entertaining for an adult, such as a 'joking' made-up story about a child, can cause tremendous long-lasting distress for that child, even after that child has reached adulthood.

Consider the situation, at the age of four I had lost my father, my shaggy dog Biddu, the day-to-day close attention from my mother and my baby sister to my grandparents, and was regularly told by my grandfather that I looked different from my family and really belonged to strangers.

I began to think, who are my real parents and why didn't they love me? Added to the trauma of the death of my father, my dog, feelings of abandonment and the emotional collapse of my mother, my grandpa's jokes about me were too much for me to make sense of.

CHAPTER 4

MY SISTER'S IMAGINARY FRIENDS

Resilience and Attachment

Gradually, I came to learn that children are resilient by nature, possessing minds flexible enough to develop the most incredible resources to serve as coping strategies to be employed in times of crisis.

My baby sister was less than a year old when my father died. She missed many of the important milestone experiences wherein children learn that they can rely on the support and love of the adults that surround them. In psychology, the regular bonding process between a child and her or his caregivers is called *Attachment*.

From recent research findings, we know the importance of *Attachment* for the healthy psychological and emotional development of children. The bond created between primary caregivers and their child is of critical importance to the child's development of both emotional resilience and the ability to create future emotional bonds.

Those bonds are required to allow the child to trust others when they reach adulthood.

Well, after my father death and my mother's sadness and depression my sister certainly didn't have the opportunity to attach to my mother. My mother was so consumed by her grief and the financial difficulties brought on by the sudden death of my father that she failed to appreciate the harm that was caused to my sister by being sent away from her immediate family to live with her grandparents. What my mother sought for my sister was a secure place, what she lost for my sister was her ability to bond with her mother and siblings.

My grandmother was a beautiful woman, inside and out, but one overshadowed by her husband, my grandfather. And while our grandparents were present for my sister, the arrangement lacked emotional support, the expression of love and focused attention on her.

Vivi, my sister's friend

So, after her first few years living with our grandparents, and when my sister was about three, she created an imaginary family. This, to provide her the love and attention she yearned for but was missing.

Vivi was her imaginary friend. My sister also created an imaginary brother for *Vivi, Mechon,* and a very loving mom and dad for Vivi and her brother. This imaginary family provided emotional support to my sister. She would talk, share stories and play with Vivi for hours on end.

Occasionally, Vivi's brother would be part of my sister's playtime with Vivi, although her relationship with Mechon was like that of a sister and an older brother. Her imaginary family became the 'grounding' in my sister's early life, as she confronted challenging years with our grandparents.

At times, my sister would invite one or her entire imaginary family for dinner, and, with me present, we would set two or three empty chairs at the table. We would speak to my sister's imaginary friends as if they were there. We would offer them food and drink, pretending to serve them dinner. In these occasions, Vivi and Mechon would provide their thoughts through my sister; she brought them into our conversations. She would convey their comments, as they were very shy. Also, as, being imaginary, they were never hungry and, accordingly, would always refuse our offers.

As my sister invented her, and just as Floridena was for me (I will introduce her later, she was real) Vivi was funny, assertive, talented, intelligent and much loved by her family. My sister's imaginary family supported her for all the years that she lived with our grandparents, separated from her mother and siblings. I later learned that my sister had assumed that she was placed with her grandparents because she must have been too much of a bother for my mother, brother and me.

For all of her early family difficulties, today, six decades later, my sister is the proud mother of three, a loving grandmother and a successful counselor. She is the knowledgeable and skillful manager of the seminars that we present monthly, providing information and teaching to others so they too can make sense of their lives and become strategists in their own life journey.

When, much later in our lives, I asked my sister about Vivi and her family, she said that, based on what she recalls and now knows about her invention of Vivi and Vivi's imaginary family, she was then likely experiencing a period of having "multiple personalities".

My sister's Vivi was loved, happy, and always having fun. Vivi was smart and could do no wrong. Vivi could talk whenever she wanted without either our Grandpa getting upset or Grandma getting into trouble (Grandpa would blame Grandma for his upsets). Vivi could have surprise visitors for dinner, something totally unacceptable for Grandpa. Most significantly, our grandparents accepted, or at least tolerated, Vivi and her family.

From what I now understand about the creation and 'lives' of my sister's imaginary friends (who first 'appeared' a few years following our father's death while living with our grandparents), they served as 'compensation' for her real losses. My sister had been sent away, emotionally abandoned by our grieving mother.

The way I see it today, love and security were absent in my grandparents' house, despite my grandmother having both the intent and desire to provide both love and security for my sister.

My grandma was too scared of the consequences if she had ever freely expressed her emotions around home; Grandpa was not a receptive audience.

So, Vivi and her imaginary family 'arrived'. She kept my sister afloat, becoming my sister's emotional support in those years of separation from us. Vivi provided my sister with necessary emotional support in the same way Floridena (again, to be introduced below) did for me during the most vulnerable years of my childhood.

Vivi was part of my sister's life for many years. We became quite accustomed to 'talk' to Vivi and her family when visiting with my sister, until one day when our aunt, who was looking after us at the time, was very busy and didn't want us to talk or play with Vivi. For my sister, the time of another separation had come, Vivi was hurt and she 'left' forever.

Later, 'missing' Vivi, I asked my sister several times why Vivi wasn't around anymore. My sister said that Vivi had been ignored in Grandpa's house, and, as a result, didn't want to be her friend anymore. Just like that, Vivi was gone.

What we call in the mental health field multiple personality disorder was probably the origin and sustenance of Vivi's time with my sister, but while 'she' was there she supported the emotional growth and resiliency that developed in my sister's life journey.

CHAPTER 5

MY OWN ANGEL

I have learned over the years that life works in very mysterious ways.

When my father died, it was time for me to begin school. I began by attending a daycare run by nuns, it was close to home. The nuns did not like me. Not only did I have red hair, but I was also left handed!

Apparently God doesn't like children to have red hair and be left-handed. Quite the combination, or so it seemed. I recall my mother debating with the nuns about my use of my left hand for writing. Their suggested solution was to tie my left hand to my back so as to force me to write with my right hand. I don't recall if they ever did that to me, and mom is no longer here to ask.

So, this remains one of my memories left hanging. Maybe, just the fear of having my left hand tied to my back did the trick and prompted me to write with my right hand. Today, I write and eat with my right hand but do everything else with my left hand.

It appears God is not that mad at me after all (maybe just a bit!).

Floridena

The first teacher I can remember very vividly is Floridena.

To this day, I have not being able to find another Floridena on this planet. For my sister, Vivi was the strength and support she needed to get through her early hard times, Floridena was there for me and at the same time.

Now, sitting in front of my computer, and having asked (to no avail) the question ". . . do you know Floridena?" what seems a million times to participants attending our seminars, still, and after fourteen years of asking, I am yet to find someone who also knows of Floridena.

I assure you, Floridena was mine, she was my earlier support. For me, she was sent to this planet to help me at the time I needed help most. I was Floridena's purpose in her life journey, my own angel sent to earth to take care of a little red hair girl with freckles and a stool, trying to reach high places to see everything around her.

Floridena was my elementary school teacher. She was there when I began school and, you are not going to believe this, she retired when I finished elementary school. Isn't that weird? I tell you, she was my own angel.

When my father died, our family disintegrated, the "baby lying on the gigantic bed" went to live with my grandparents while my brother and I stayed with the "sobbing woman. Our father figure was replaced by our grandpa, a resentful and angry man that did not want the responsibilities that come with a young family, especially any responsibility for a red hair girl that carried a stool to reach higher places. My freckles and a strong will that stood out from the other children in the neighbourhood were, definitively, not appealing to Grandpa.

I was, and am, different than my brother and sister in regard to our physical characteristics. As is typical in a Latin American family, my brother has dark hair and black eyes while my sister has light brown hair but also dark eyes. Not me, here I was with bright orange hair, big brown freckles and sparkly green-yellow eyes!

At four years old, you never question or doubt what adults tell you. It is my belief that fibbing is not part of a child's mindset at that age. I cannot prove it, but I can certainly speak about it. A story told by an adult, about who you are or where you came from, was taken as being true by a child. The concept of a "joke" or fibbing is not clear to children of young age.

My grandpa created what he considered a funny story about me and my origins. While his story became, or at least seemed to me to be, the joke of our family, for me the events he reported were so real that it was very hurtful, at least until I met Floridena.

And, I was not 'different' just to my family; I was different to, seemingly, everyone. At school, my classmates also made sure that I knew the differences; I was an orange spot around them, a carrot head with a 'poopy' (spotted) face.

Then, one day Floridena told me another story.

While I cannot recall when "the story" became my salvation, when I adopted it as mine, or how it became my strength through the most difficult years of my life, I can say that the story allowed me to survive Grandpa, the sobbing woman and teasing classmates. Floridena's story also ended my confusion about my life and, somehow, answered my questions as to who really cared about me.

Floridena called me "my little angel". Maybe she had found me crying in a corner, not playing with the other girls, being teased or being sad, and having retreated to be quiet by myself. Whatever prompted her to approach me that day with her story, one that replaced in importance Grandpa's hurtful story and ended my fear of my classmate's teasing, I am not sure, but I certainly remember what she said as if she just said it today:

> *Irene, you are a little angel with a big and red ponytail . . . and you know why your ponytail is red? . . . well God is a very busy man . . . he loves you very much and when he looks down . . . he sees right away that ponytail and finds you . . . and he knows you are OK!*
>
> *Do you know why the freckles? Because at night those freckles transform into bright little lights, and when God is checking up on you . . . He does it with no trouble!!*

Talking about a strategy for facing life!!

That story was my salvation for many years, right up until I was old enough to realize it was only a nice story. That story, told by a kind teacher, somehow allowed me to survive a critical period of my life, living in a very negative environment with a 'sobbing' mother and a grumpy resentful grandpa.

The reality was that my mother was so consumed with her pain and sorrow that she did not have time (or even the awareness) to be a nurturing and supportive mother for us. In those days, the idea of admitting being depressed or seeking help was not even an option.

I decided (with my "red ponytail and freckled face") not to tell anybody what Floridena had confided to me. From then on, I was so excited with my new knowledge I could not be still. Every day, with my red hair in a ponytail and holding up my four year old face to the sky, head held high, I would walk to school looking up (so God would not have any trouble finding me and knowing I was the best little girl on the planet!).

Thereafter, when the conversation about "who I was" was brought up by grandpa at the dinner table, I could hardly contain my excitement Wow!!! The sobbing woman and my dad had no idea who they had found in the garbage can! And, as to you, Grandpa, I am not telling you who I am!!! I am not giving you the satisfaction of knowing that you are sitting beside a little angel!!

From then on, in my head everyone that came to me was lucky. No longer did I care if the other girls rejected me, laughed at me, teased me. Nobody, other than me and my Floridena, knew the secret of who I was. That confidence was enough to keep me going while my mother was dealing with her own pain and grief.

For many years after Floridena retired and I had moved on to another school, I loved and treasured the story. Even when my life was not easy, I learned to trust my angelical side, knowing that I had to move on, in the same way Floridena was moving on with her life.

Today, when I teach people about the importance of the significant memories of their lives, there are two types of memories I emphasize—the ones that build your confidence, and the ones that can destroy your confidence and create dysfunction in your life.

Going back in time and "mending" those defective memories allows people to 'rewire' their minds and create other and more sustaining memories towards enjoying a more fulfilling life. We are not our past, but since we rely so much on it if we do not rearrange the wiring in our brains, the 'faulty wiring' will not allow us to create healthy connections here in 'the present'. The present is and should be our gift for the day!

What I learned looking back at the experiences of my grandpa and Floridena, is that in life there are two different kinds of people. First are the ones that leave a positive legacy of helpful memories for others, they are to be remembered forever for their contributions to our lives. The other type of person has no intention to support, help, or even be concerned. They fail to make a positive impact in the life journeys of others.

When they leave the scene, they could well ask themselves what was the purpose of their having been on this planet; there may be nothing good for them to remember, or, of them, for the people they leave behind.

When I work with women in my seminars, I always ask them where are they in their relationships with others. How do they want to be remembered: as a Floridena or as my Grandpa?

We all have the opportunity to choose how we want to impact this world and those that live in it. We need to decide how we want to be remembered. We can impact somebody's life either in a positive or a negative way. Attitude has no cost, it is free, and when you invest in having a good attitude the outcomes in your life for others and for you are exponentially good.

What I have learned over the years is that the ability to develop life strategies that can and will sustain you arises in part from our ability to rearrange our past history. We are not our past, and we don't need to keep going back to behaviors and emotions of what was, especially when they are connected with negative feelings.

Every day, we can start fresh and create new positive memories and feelings. If we learn from our past experiences and let go of the past when those memories are harmful, our mind can take care of the needed new rewiring!!

CHAPTER 6

MY BROTHER

What about him?

The only time I remember my brother crying came after I told him of our dad's passing. Other than then, I remember his childhood as having been, at least outwardly, very happy. I recall his inventing things, bicycling and roller blading.

But, now thinking more deeply about him and then, I don't know if he was always happy or he was hiding his feelings, perhaps a bit of both.

As an adult, he is a very sensitive guy, his eyes tear up for anything that brings his emotions to the surface. He is still as funny as he was on occasion when a kid. Cracking jokes, gently teasing, and converting the simplest life events into the funniest stories—your jaws can hurt from laughing so much.

One of the things we used to get in trouble over when we were kids had to do with my younger sister, who, after a lengthy stay at our grandparent's home, had been returned to us. She would cry (sometimes for no apparent reason), and when she did my mom would be after us, my brother and me, regardless whether it was our fault or not.

One day, my sister was crying in her room and my brother and I were trying to convince her to stop. Our mother was about to come home, so both of us were going to be in big trouble if she found her crying. I was sitting on my sister's bed rubbing her back and talking to her, trying to get her to stop crying. My brother, as always, and as he was talking to her, was playing, this time with a ball of yarn.

He tied it to the end of the bed, then to the lamp and back to the bed, then to the light switch and to the closet's handles. The three of us were in that small room, with the yarn passed through all the furniture and around us many times. Suddenly he stopped what he was doing and yelled ". . . *when I turn the light switch on . . . we are all going to blow up and die!.*"

My little sister jumped out of bed and clutched me, landing on my lap. At the same time, I also tried to escape from the yarn that was wound over our bodies and the room. We were all screaming like pigs trying to get out of their pen when my mother walked into the room. My brother got in BIG TROUBLE over that incident.

That was my brother, easy going and always making jokes, then as a child and later as a teenager. Now, today, he is a loving husband, a great dad and grandfather. It sometimes appears that life for him is a joke and he is going to try to his best to live it that way.

While we were growing up, he was always very resourceful. He managed to get money, a commodity always in short supply in our home. He did by tasks, such as helping my uncle clean his car, helping around his house and carrying groceries into the house.

My brother was my mother's favourite. My sister and I knew and accepted it as our reality. My mother and brother could be together for a full day, a day comprised solely by their conversations on various topics. They loved each other's company. The ease of their relationship was likely due to my brother's easy going nature, which allowed my mother to enjoy him more.

When my mother had aged and was very ill, the time came that I had the intuition that she was not going to be around for too much longer. I asked my brother to go on a holiday with her. He did, even when at that time our mother had slowed down and was quite dependent on him to get around. Nevertheless, they had the time of their lives.

My mother died a few months later, and we (my siblings and me) agreed that the trip couldn't have come a better time, providing her the best ending of her life. For her life celebration we shared with those attending the following letter.

It reflects my mother's nature and, as well, her preference for my brother.

Celebrating the life of Adriana.

Adriana had a long life, one full of talents and barriers at the same time. She was able to overcome all of them, and she was very proud of her accomplishments. She was a fighter, a woman with courage.

She was born in 1923, the older daughter of a family of four. She was athletic, an excellent swimmer and very active all her life. She married young but had a short time with her life partner. She had three children, each forever in love with her even when the words were seldom said; we all stayed around her all our lives.

My brother was her favourite . . . there was nothing that he could do that was wrong. His picture was kept in the front of my mother's wallet, while those of my sister and I lay behind all kinds of other papers filling her wallet.

My brother knew how to get my mother's affection. He would tape her favorite shows, and they would sit and watch TV in Spanish. He would play the music that she liked, and she would take him to places she enjoyed; they would talk for hours about UFO's and the past cultures that have influenced our world, such as the Mayas.

Even when my mother was acting very head strong, my sister-in-law was aware of how to gain her respect. She was very attentive to our mother's needs, and prepared the meals she enjoyed, and shared her time with her husband, our mother's son, with her with no limits.

Adriana was very protective of her family. Anybody that approached her clan (which extended to boyfriends, husbands, wives and friends), she would look at them with a hard face and refuse to allow them into her world.

She became a widow at 29, left with three babies to fight with no resources and very little skills. She never married again and turned her family into her pride. We all completed our studies and moved on to better lives, after the initial struggles.

My mother always wanted to maintain her authority and control over us. My sister and I always reacted by fighting and arguing with her, but my brother, her preferred one, was a better psychologist than my sister and I together. He learned to ignore her and avoid fights.

As my mother was getting older, she learned to enjoy her family more, and to give thanks for all of the gifts she received in life.

*We celebrate your life Adriana . . . and we want to
let you know that the seeds that you planted grew
in fertile soil. We are healthy, happy and loved,
and we will continue planting those same seeds
in the future generations to come.*

We love you, and we will see you in eternity.

Your son and daughters.

After our mother died, we three siblings came to be better able
to understand her life, allowing us to enjoy memories of her, for
the 'gifts' she gave and still are giving us, and for what she was.

When we stopped trying to change her and, instead, changed
our approach to her, we began to better understand who she
was and what her mission in life was. Many time we waste so
much time faulting our beginning or our past rather than taking
the short cut and making sense of our past and leaving it as the
past!.

CHAPTER 7

BACK ON THE ROLLER COASTER!

Those first few years of my life are foggy; yet, I can recall vivid scenes in my memory of a baby (my sister), my older brother, the sobbing woman (my mother), grandparents, aunts and uncles, children from my school, Vivi and Floridena. The memories made more sense to me later in life, as through concentrated reflection I was able to connect the memories together into a coherent picture. I began to make sense of my personal journey.

After Floridena and elementary school, I moved on to a Junior High school. I was very excited since I understood that I was now a big girl and I would be going to a school with lots of teachers. My excitement was largely about the prospects of finding other Floridenas in the new school.

But, that did not happen, although I have memories of good teachers, funny teachers, serious teachers, bad teachers, none impacted my life as much as Floridena did. I guess she was the only one sent to me to allow me to jump start my life after the initial difficult years of my childhood.

Without Floridena, I went back to being the 'troubled girl'. Defiant, rebellious, a poor student, always behind and having to catch up, never on time; once again that description became me. At home, even when my mother was physically present, we were on our own in regards to going to school.

We were responsible for many tasks, including getting ready and going to school, doing our homework, and preparing breakfast. Our mother was never the same after the death of our father. An experience like that can leave you devastated, and for a long time, if not forever. That is, unless you are consciously working on recovering your memories, and overcoming the feelings that arise from the memories, those of anguish and abandonment.

I cannot say I was a good student, or even that I applied myself to school work, that is until I was in the final three years of high school. By then, I had become aware that if I wanted to continue to higher education I had to do better. My performance in the final years of secondary (high) school was vital for me to have an opportunity to move on to higher education. This was particularly the case since I was coming from a public school. In Chile, then, there was little chance of someone from a public high school entering university.

Achieving a full awareness of my past and creating a vision of who I am and what I wanted to do with my life led to my decisions to change both my approach and direction in life. The process involved a combination of 'seeing' myself in the future, visualizing my mother struggling through life and not wanting to be like her, recognizing my desire to have more material things (such as new shoes that fit me, nice dresses that don't either hang on me or have to last for a long time), being self-sufficient and independent, and never being abandoned and left without resources.

At that time, I was thinking, reflecting on, that I had been abandoned by two important people in my early life, first my father and then Floridena, left to struggle on my own.

When I made the decision to become a good student, change for the better came instantly. That is why I know by my own experience (from when I was as a young girl) that when someone wants to change, first they need to think about their past and their opportunities and then make up their mind to change. If the change makes sense, then become fully committed to bringing it about. Positive results can begin to happen right away.

If you become aware and are committed, neither time, a place or a person can or should deter your conviction to change. A clearer picture of what happens in the brain once one makes a decision is set out by Dr. Dispenza (2012)[1]. He explains the neurological process involved in making a decision to change, and how one's brain immediately begins to rewire its connections.

Improvement

I became and remained an honour student from grade ten on. Coming from having received almost failing grades in previous

---

[1]   Dr. J. Dispenza (2012) Breaking the Habit of Being Yourself.

years, I became one of the top three students in my classes. My turn-around for the better was such a surprise for my teachers and the school's administrators that it was regularly discussed in teachers' assembly; I came under observation for those three years of high school.

The initial view of my teachers was that I was cheating and that they needed to find out how I was managing to obtain such good grades. They didn't understand that I had 'changed my mind' as to who I wanted to be and was beginning to take control of my life. This beneficial process took place even ahead of my full awareness of what I was doing. At that time, I did not know the power that resided in my mind to bring about a transformation.

Although a full awareness of my discovery awaited more time and reflection, what I had learned at that time of my life was the power of the human will. I had decided to change, by first reflecting on my experiences in life, and then determining what I wanted for my future.

In the final analysis, it was my choice to create other outcomes for myself than what awaited me if I continued with my prior attitudes and behavior.

I was only fourteen years old, and I had no idea of the power of the will and of intention. I did not think about 'the how', I just made the decision to change, and that decision moved me to take many positive actions that improved my life.

When I look back, I realize that, then, I didn't know the capacity I had to change my future, and that positive results would flow simply by changing my way of thinking and, then, my behaviors.

My own experience with making changes helped me to realize the importance of learning about the brain, its processes, capabilities, its potential, and the power that resides in one's will.

I began to produce positive results. At the time, I didn't at first even relate to what I was doing different. In my mind, my luck had changed. It seems funny how I was not then able to fully appreciate that the new results arose because I had made changes. I was getting along better with my teachers, I was asking questions, I was focused, and I was asking the good students in the class for help.

I didn't realize until later that my new friends were not the same as my old friends. I began to stick around the higher achievers and no longer hang around with trouble-makers. Yet, my thinking was still distorted, at that point I did not 'own' the changes I had made. In my awareness at the time, for once my luck had changed, and I would 'ride' with it for as long as I could.

Now when I look back, I appreciate more how relatively small changes in behavior can bring amazing results, even when you don't have full awareness of what has taken place and haven't taken responsibility for those changes.

Today, in my practice, I point out to seminar participants the importance of first taking small steps towards the direction they want to move in their lives. And, I advise them that as they make those small changes, those changes will become the motivator for other small changes. The ripple effect moves you forward toward the direction you have set for yourself for your journey in life.

I used to perceive my early life as one where my family had been struck by sudden bad luck when my father died. However, years later and now an adult, I realize that my father should assume some responsibility for our struggles. Because he never took sufficient care of his health, he died, leaving behind a dependent woman with three small children and few resources.

I cannot remember where I read this, but it makes a lot of sense: *"The thoughts you are having today about your life will become a reality in two years' time."*

CHAPTER 8

ANOTHER LUCKY EVENT?

When I finished high school, with good grades, I was ready to venture into a new world. Historically (in my country), entry into university was reserved for students coming from private schools, with the financial resources to allow them to prepare for the national exam that, in essence, determined career opportunities.

Entrance into university programs leading to professional careers required a high score in the national exam. Higher scores provided access to careers such as Medicine, Law, Psychology and Dentistry. Statistically, it was a proven fact that those that had graduated from private schools dominated as to the number of entrants into university level education.

I knew, coming from the public school system and a poor family, that I had very little chance to obtain a university education. If I tried to get in and wrote the entrance exams, I would be competing with students from private schools, students with tutors, students that would have completed pre-university courses (preparing them for the national exam).

In general, I would be competing with students that would have a better understanding of their capabilities and potential that I had as for myself at that point.

To enter university, I needed to not only pass the National Exam but get the high scores needed to qualify for entrance to programs leading to a professional career. To increase the chance to receive a good score, there were educational institutes that provided training and support for high school graduates. My mother could not afford to send me to such an institute.

And, while my grades from high school we're good, they were insufficient to provide me with confidence as to my capabilities. My fear was that my good grades were based on me having been 'lucky' in my final three years of schooling. It didn't occur to me that I was intelligent and capable, and that I had changed the direction of my life by becoming more focused on what I did not wanted to be. While luck was not the reason for my recent success, I was yet to form the vision of me as a person with skills and abilities.

Without the advantage of having attended an institute to improve my chances at the national examination, I wrote the exams. To my great surprise, my score in the National Exam was at the 90th percentile, I had scored in the top ten percent of those that had taken the exam. I was beside myself, not knowing what to think at that moment. It had never occurred to me that I was that capable.

Now, I had to accept that I was bright, and that my efforts in high school had paid off.

My happiness and excitement was short lived, at least initially. Unfortunately, I began to think that "somebody" had made a mistake and my reported high score was due to a computer glitch. I began to panic, thinking sooner or later the mistake would be discovered.

My thoughts were running wild. What if the mistake takes a long time to be discovered? What if I enter a program leading to a professional career and finish it without being discovered, only to be discovered and dismissed after being in a career? Or, what if they find out earlier and I am to be discharged from the University for dishonesty?

What I learned from that experience is that the set of my beliefs that were present in my life at that time were not supporting me, not at all. Then, I was convinced I did not have any potential or talents, and whatever happened to me was the result of being either lucky or unlucky, there could be no other explanation.

I have also come to understand that my view of myself, at that time, was partially due to the fact that, other than Floridena, I did not have any adequate role models or mentors in my life, those that would have helped me to think otherwise. Everything for me was external; sometimes I was lucky, sometimes my luck would run out. And, if bad luck occurred, I would be left 'on the wrong side of the street'.

Thinking back, I wish I could have had somebody like *Floridena* beside me all the time, helping me to think my life through, encouraging me to grow up with a set of beliefs that supported me, rather than my holding to ideas that provided an underlying anxiety all the time.

Now, In my present work putting on empowerment seminars, I go back to my life's experiences over and over, thinking about what I was missing in my early life, this so I can make sure that the "next me", not the me of my past, is present, taking full responsibility for the outcomes in the now and into the future.

My luck is running out!

At the age of seventeen, I had completed high school (with decent grades) and was ready to enter university (assuming I could get through the entrance examinations). So, against the odds I passed the exam and got into the university.

I didn't choose Psychology as a career, Psychology chose me. Actually, it was the first faculty department to accept my application, and I was not going to wait around for another field offering a career—for me, "I was lucky" that I had one.

But locked in my dysfunctional set of beliefs, I still felt that my luck would soon run out. I was convinced that the minute that my classmates or professors knew who I 'really' was, they would know "I was a fake" and that I didn't belong in classes full of students of great intelligence and ample resources.

At the time, the percentage of university students coming from Chile's lower socio-economic class was almost nil. University mostly belonged to people coming from well-off families with important 'last names', definitively not the place for a *red haired girl with lots of freckles* coming from public school.

In order to survive the University before being caught, I developed a plan, a very sick plan as I evaluated it later. I was to be "incognito" to all my professors and classmates. I was going to graduate as a Psychologist without anyone knowing who I was. In my plan, I would arrive late for classes, so nobody would pay any attention to me. I would sit at the back of the class, and keep my mouth shut (no one was to know I was there!).

I began my education towards a career in Psychology by putting my plan into place. I met a group of women in my class that seemed quiet and were into studying; I didn't think being among them, studying with them, would be dangerous. We began to study together, and since I was to always be *incognito*, I took on the task of reading all the assigned books and articles, and preparing summaries and notes for everyone in the group.

The understanding was that if a presentation to the class was involved, I wouldn't do it, and that task would be handled by another.

My view of myself was so dysfunctional that even the good grades I achieved in my classes didn't alert me to my potential. Again, for every good grade I received, the cause was either luck or a mistake from the professor grading my submissions.

Over the past years, discussing the topic of incorrectly perceived personas with my seminar participants, I discovered that many of them had experienced similar feelings. Beliefs can be stronger than facts. The sufferer finds the way, dysfunctional as it is, to validate their invalid beliefs, despite the facts that 'stand' in front of them!

I knew my luck was running out when, in my second year in Psychology, one of the assignments in an advanced class was "to interview patients". My initial plan to go *incognito* had worked 'perfectly' for almost two years. I arrived late to classes, left before everyone else, studied with a very quiet group and avoided any type of group activity that involved my giving a presentation. I always took a "back stage job", such as researching, preparing materials, or creating presentations for someone else in the study group to give.

But this time, I had to interview a patient and come up with a diagnosis. Two years into a career as *an incognito* psychologist in training, keeping with my plan was proving not to be an easy task! Being incognito in front of a patient was impossible. My fears at that time were larger than my desire to be a Psychologist, when the time came for me to interview a patient, I couldn't do it.

> I sat in my professor's office waiting for the patient selected for my assignment to arrive. She came into the office and asked me if I was the interviewer. My heart was racing so hard that I could hardly speak, I was shaking, my voice was almost breaking. I remember saying: "*I am*

*waiting for her too, but don't worry, you can see
her now. I will come back later."*

As I left, I felt it was the end of my career. I had run out of strategies to be invisible, and I could no longer hide from the truth.

CHAPTER 9

MY NIGHTMARE AND ITS END

Picture me, going to classes every day, making sure I was invisible. I constantly had nightmares about it. When going to class, my mouth was dry. I had stomach aches constantly, and my heart raced every time I thought even about the possibility of being 'discovered'.

I had a very dysfunctional belief, don't you think? But it was real and present every day for two years! The memories about those days remain very clear. I wanted to stop the pain and pressure, I wanted to quit university. But, the thought of my family, of me not having a better future, these thoughts were also devastating.

I was the first one of my generation in our extended family to enter university. My mom was counting on me to help my brother and sister after I graduated and was in my career. My mother hoped that everything would change for our family once I graduated.

In the previous two years, I had tried many times to raise my hand in class, make *an intelligent* comment, or ask *an intelligent* question. I was unable to do so. I feared that my heart would stop, or I would faint and have a heart attack and die on the spot!

After the *interview* incident with the patient, I was certain it was the end of my career, the end of any hope of becoming a Psychologist. I decided I had to find a way to 'end it all'. I could not bear the thought of seeing the face of my mother if I was to tell her I was quitting university. So, I created a "master plan", a very disturbing master plan.

I was convinced that if I ever faced my fear, my heart would suddenly stop and I would have a massive heart attack and die. With that image in my head, I decided to stage an honourable death; I decided to face the class by being a spokesperson at the next opportunity our study group had to make a presentation. When I announced my decision to my women's group, they all looked at me with puzzled faces but said nothing.

The opportunity quickly came, a group assignment requiring a presentation on Theories and System in Psychology. The professor was a very demanding man that walked around campus as if he was the most important person in the world and his class was the most interesting in the universe. So, if a student didn't make a perfect presentation, or worse, didn't know the content, he was brutal.

In my then-sick mind, taking on the presentation, collapsing and dying doing it was better than quitting. In my distorted thinking It would be over, and sooner rather than later. I began to get ready to execute my plan. My effort had to look real, so I began to study, memorizing as much of the presentation as I could.

I worked out every detail of the presentation and how I would play it out. I visualized myself arriving at class, having all my notes in front of me, beginning my presentation and, shortly after, collapsing in a fashionable way so that everyone, including my mother, would be impressed as to how hard I had worked. They would all know that I had worked so hard that my studying had killed me!!

Thinking about it now, my mind was a sick mind in action. And yet, I did not have a mental health issue at that point in my life (or, did I?). I looked very normal, although my distorted beliefs were totally irrational no one could see them!

I have learned over the years that many of us carry distortions of reality without even doubting the veracity of the view, while 'walking around' looking definitively normal.

Since I wanted my 'departure' to be real, honourable and dignified, I decided not to eat for a couple of days ahead of the presentation. I didn't want to vomit before collapsing in front of the class. I didn't want to look gross, with my clothes stained by undigested food from the previous day. Then, under the same pretext, I stopped drinking water. This, so if I vomited it would only be a little trail of water running down the side of my mouth.

Very dignified and honourable, don't you think?

Well, eventually the time came for my end; the day of the presentation was in front of me. I went into the bathroom many times before the presentation. I was gagging, feeling sick, no surprise given what loomed ahead and the fact that I had nothing in my stomach. By this time I was dizzy, not having either eaten or had drunk water for a couple of days. I walked into class almost fainting, but ready to go.

I was not going to stop now, so close to the end of my nightmare.

By now, you probably have guessed I did not die. If I had, I wouldn't be here, facing my computer and writing about it!

On that day, I stood in front of the class for the first time, then two years into my university courses. I assure you, up to the moment I stood in front of the class and our professor, my plan was working. Many of my fellow students didn't even know I was a member of the class. Thankfully, standing in front of the class, I couldn't see faces or hear voices. It was like I was alone in the middle of a desert.

I began my presentation, waiting and expecting I would faint and my heart would stop at any minute. Then, all of a sudden, I became a different person. I didn't know it was me. I came out of that unfeeling, unaware of others, state. I 'woke up' in the presence of a large number of students and my professor, delivering a presentation.

The most impressive part of my initial classroom experience was the clarity, knowledge, confidence, compassion and other feelings that were then displayed during and after my presentation. I cannot properly describe the extent and depth of the collage of 'feelings' I experienced. I awoke in the classroom in a *new zone, one* I had never experienced before. Initially, I didn't know if it was real or not.

My mind was totally clear, and I could see everyone in front of me.

Today, some forty years later, I still remember the topic, the words, and the references, the faces of the students and the professor, and all the steps that took me to that moment.

I lost my fear on the spot. My mind opened, my heart began to regain control, and my vision cleared. I no longer felt like gagging, and I could remember everything that I studied. I spoke to the class of facts, naming authors and journal references, and provided my views on the topic of my presentation and as to the discussions provided in the literature on my subject matter.

I was lecturing, and, if I may say, probably even better than my professor!!

I imagine that if someone there in that classroom at that time had asked me about the nuclear diffusion of the atom, a subject I know little about, I was on such a 'roll' that I would have sounded so knowledgeable that my classmates and professor would have fainted on the spot!

I wish you could visualize the scene. I was standing, surprisingly composed, in front of a group of students I really didn't know, nor did they really know me. Fear conquered!! If you cannot visualize it, at least I can try to describe what the scene likely 'looked like' for them.

For most of the class, this was the first time they were aware of me. Maybe, some of them thought I was an invited professor (Ha! Ha!). Mouths were open; my classmates were looking around, elbowing each other, raising eyebrows, and asking their seat mates who I was. Some of them did not even know that I existed, and had been in the same class with them for two years!

When I was done, I stood stunned. While I didn't truly 'recognize' the presenter as me, it certainly was me. My first presentation remains one of my most memorable experiences and another one of those amazing AHA! moments in my life. Before that experience, I wasn't aware of what I was capable of.

That experience changed my life: I had faced my fears and false beliefs, and, for the first time, I realized what I was capable of doing. The experience was an epiphany.

Later, after continuing and completing my studies, I came to understood what had happened that day.

I had forced my brain to confront and pass the critical point of fear. We all can do that, but we need to be prepared to suffer the pre-symptoms. In addition, I believe there is something bigger than us. If we are willing to surrender to it (that bigger place, energy, universe, higher power, or GOD), we will be able to find answers that otherwise would be beyond us.

From that experience, I learned that whatever I may face I cannot predict either my reaction or the outcome. I learned that at up to that time my life was being driven by fear, insecurity and a core set of beliefs that were not supporting me. Fears, limitations, anguish and despair were part of my psyche. My psyche was filled with the 'cannot', I am less than, I am a failure at, I cannot do it, I don't belong, I am stupid.

Notwithstanding the importance of my psychological 'rebirth', I was and still am saddened by the fact that I lost two years of a better life, one embracing and overcoming fear, insecurities and the desire to escape from reality. That said I am aware that before my epiphany I didn't know what lay behind my fears and insecurity. Accordingly, I couldn't then understand cognitively what was going on, and I didn't know how to reframe my perceptions.

Knowledge is power, and I wish I had that power from the onset of my life. As to why no one taught me earlier about brain functioning, its potential, and what happens to us when we lock it into a fear position, few if any around me knew of such matters.

And, from when I began studying psychology, my objective was to allow me to be able to help people like me. However, for the first two years of my studies, I didn't know how to help myself, either as to how to create a way out of my fears and insecurities.

Many years later, in Canada and doing post graduate studies in Psychology, I learned what had happened to me that day, when *my dysfunctional master plan*—that I expected would end with my death—did not work.

I have learned that, in those first two years in class and ahead of the presentation that led to relief, I was constantly living under the 'stress response'. I was assessing my environment as being threatening and, accordingly, I always had my body and brain in the state of 'fight or flight'. That response doesn't allow for the utilization of the full capacity of the brain. For two years I was working with less than 20% of my brain capacity and I was still doing well!. I was high-jacked by my brain's limbic system, the primitive part of the brain which functions to protect us.

I was consumed by fears about the world, being found out, being a disappointment to others, not belonging, not being intelligent enough, being embarrassed, being expelled. I was always expecting the worst to happen.

Ahead of my presentation, I was hiding and trying to be invisible, invisibility being my dysfunctional way to address my fears.

Dr. Dispenza[2] wrote: *"Living in survival causes us to focus on the .00001 percent, instead of the 99.99999 percent of reality."*

After my presentation experience, I began to work with the unknown part of me. Until then, and although I was studying Psychology, I didn't know how to begin to work against my fears of being judged, feeling inadequate and being unacceptable.

---

[2]   J. Dispenza.(2012) Breaking the Habit of Being Yourself

I was working on my own, but, at least, after the *presentation* experience I could relax and begin to walk the unknown. Now my understanding became I have an unknown potential that unless allowed to come out I would never know how far it could take me.

I was both thrilled and intrigued by my classroom experience, it changed my outlook as to my potentiality, and possibilities that lie in me and in others that could move us forward (if allowed).

CHAPTER 10

LIFE IS GOOD AGAIN

Life is never dull.

The roller-coaster of life has a habit of turning and twisting in the most incredible ways. We have many opportunities to transform our lives anyway we want, and yet we still find ways of limiting ourselves.

My desire to learn more as to how to overcome obstacles has, since my university presentation experience, always been at the back of my mind. I began to observe 'life', knowing that there was far more 'out there' than what I had experienced.

When I was closer to finishing my first degree, I met my wonderful life partner (of 43 years now). When I graduated as a Psychologist, I also gave birth to our first son, Daniel.

The arrival of our first son made me even more aware of the importance of my search to find the best of me, so as to allow me to be the best I can for my growing family. While I had absorbed considerable knowledge, I was still not sure how to "transform people's lives", and how I was going to help my son in displaying his potential without fears

I went to work, carrying on for many years in the area of Psychology still being aware that what I knew was not enough. My search for meaning (that resides in all aspects of life) and my concurrent desire to find the best way to understand not only the road blocks that we construct in our minds but also how to clear them, has been an abiding interest in my career.

After another birth of my second son, Andre, I continued with my search and becoming a loving, nurturing, resourceful parents was one of my most important goals in life. We now had two beautiful boys, then I gave in to a continuing desire to study more and we moved to Canada so I could continue my search for knowledge. My intention was to go to post graduate school and learn more about the mysteries of life. It was then that I became an avid reader of the literature of brain development, research in learning, and the Psychology of Peak Performers.

My desire to both become a better person and help others took me in several directions, from reading the results of researchers in the field of Psychology to reviewing the works of inspirational writers. I became an avid reader and follower of Wayne Dyer, Bruce Lipton, Jack Canfield and Joe Dispenza. All these authors are interested in the potentiality of the human race. Their own unique writing styles provide different perspectives on human potentiality, from the field of genetics to spirituality.

As I continued reading and thinking about the challenges faced by those living lives marked by personal road blocks and limiting beliefs, as had been my situation, I discovered opportunities to not only help others but also myself.

I went back to university and, with great difficulty, completed a Master in Psychology. (Since English is my second language, writing in English has been a challenge throughout my career.) After graduating with a Master in Psychology, it took me about ten more years to build up enough courage to pursue a Doctoral Degree, which I succeeded in doing,

Despite all this formal learning, I didn't know I was yet to learn the biggest lesson of my life.

CHAPTER 11

MASTER AND DOCTORATE (NANCY, 'GRANDPA' AND DEANNA)

By this time in my life's journey, I finally had confidence as to what I could achieve. I had created several strategies to avoid my own mental traps, and was becoming more aware of the negative 'voices' (including those generated by my own mind) that constrained me.

I grew to understand that I could overcome and transform negative voices by recalling and validating my achievements. I knew I could accomplish more, and understood that I had to move further forward, rather than 'sitting still on the sidelines' of life, observing not acting, being overwhelmed by doubts.

Thinking again about *Floridena,* my sage from my childhood, I found a professor in my master's program that helped me to not only get through that part of my education but also to face my fear of working and writing in English. Developing an ability to express my thoughts in English in a coherent and structured way proved a major challenge. Importantly, she took the time to get to know me, and to understand that my broad knowledge base was buried under my limited skills to express myself in, for me, another language, English.

I entered the master program on a probationary status, probationary because the department head (of Psychology) was not sure if the barriers to expressing myself well were related to the-then language limitation, or involved deficiencies in the knowledge areas of Psychology.

If it wasn't for that caring professor, Nancy, my new Floridena, probably I would not have lasted in the program. As it was, I graduated with a Master degree in Psychology, then promising myself never to go back to school.

Honouring that promise to myself, once again I returned to working full-time, but not for long.

Despite my initial resistance to taking more formal training, after some time working I began to think again about going back for more schooling to achieve a doctorate. While my motivation to do so was rather weak at the start, the idea was firmly planted in the 'back of my mind', and, knowing me, I knew it was not going to disappear from my consciousness.

So, I decided to apply to enter a Doctoral Program. In doing so, I ignored the recommendation of the university's Psychology department to take additional statistical courses before applying. Instead, I made a special petition to the University (from which

I had obtained the Master degree) to enroll in its Doctoral Program.

When I applied, I half hoped I would not be accepted. In my then-dysfunctional thinking, somehow showing up from time to time, if I was refused I would be able to blame the University. Going further, I could blame the University for not having the career I wanted. To my great surprise I was accepted, and without any reference to the initial recommendation to first take more statistical courses.

However, this time I didn't find another Floridena, someone to support and help me, I found another Grandpa. Upon beginning my doctoral program, I was assigned an advisor that made sure I understood very clearly what he considered my limitations. For him, I was a woman working with a second language, an impediment he made sure 'counted'.

In the end, and after 178 revisions of my dissertation, a process that involved countless nights without sleep, I was able to escape his hands relatively unharmed, with a doctorate in Psychology.

Even though I was able to complete the program, the process, the work, the relationship with my advisor, took a lot out of me. For about a year after I had successfully completed the program, I was unable to look at my dissertation, which otherwise sat, ignored, on a book shelve, without crying and feeling stressed.

Eventually, the 'pain' I incurred due to the process subsided, and I realized that I had expanded my knowledge base and now had an amazing set of new life strategies that could be used to help others, to teach them how to become the strategist in and of their own lives.

Today, long after that experience, I can attest more to the concept of the mind and body connection. Working all the time under stress, by the end of my doctoral program I had damaged my upper arms, this due to typing for long hours under severe stress. My rotator tendons in my upper arms were so damaged that in the cold Canadian winters, when my arms most hurt, the pain still brings memories of not only the academic success I enjoyed but also of the price I had to pay to reach my goals.

I knew then that just as I had overcome a grueling undertaking in the doctoral program, I could overcome 'anything'. Too many of us do not take the opportunity to ponder on the challenges conquered to get where we are, let alone reflect on the fears yet to be conquered to get where we want to be.

In writing and re-writing, my dissertation I met a wonderful woman, Deanna, who helped me with my English, particularly by editing my dissertation. Deanna was not just my "English proficiency checker"; she also helped me maintain my mental and physical strength through the doctoral program. We used to have long conversations on how I could support myself emotionally, as well as physically, in such difficult times.

She had learned similar lessons earlier in her life. She had been an independent woman who wanted to prove to the world that she didn't need anyone. She was a successful Executive Assistant until, one day, she could no longer walk, move her body or use her hands (all due to severe arthritis).

Almost overnight, Deanna went from being a fiercely fully independent and successful woman to being bound to a wheelchair, totally dependent on others even for the most private of tasks. She was my inspiration and brought me courage, she was my 'rock', when I needed her the most.

I learned through the strenuous doctorate program that I was resilient, and would not allow anyone to break my spirit. Even when I sensed negativity around me, I was able to stand and continue facing the challenges life, and the program, brought.

In order to maintain my resilience, I had to work diligently to both create more strategies that worked, and, as well, surround myself with positive women. When adversity was at its worst, I had to fight to overcome it. I created in myself a mindset that proved sufficient to overcome the negativity I endured throughout the writing of my dissertation.

Seeking ways for me to survive my journey through the doctoral program, Deanna and I created a women's support group. The group's primary purpose was to provide and receive encouragement to all members of the group, while we developed effective strategies to face the hurdles that stood in our way to achieve our goals.

We each invited friends, and we met on a regular basis. We neither had a concrete theme nor a set agenda for our gatherings. Despite that, the group 'worked'. Each of us understood the usefulness that came with supporting, creating strength, and validating our efforts.

Many of the strategies I had learned through my academic efforts were validated through group discussion. And, our group allowed me to clarify my vision of helping other women. In my plan, the initial help I could provide would come from helping women to learn how to overcome not only their fears but also how to avoid being trapped in a set of beliefs that either slows or breaks one down. The process I had in mind would lead women seeking help to the realization that the limitations that were restraining them were, in the final analysis, 'only in their head'.

It is not important to your recovery to know exactly when somebody implanted negative ideas of your limitations in your head. And, likely, many times the limitations were not set out by someone, perhaps a family member or a boss, with the intention to make you weak. Generally, it is us that transform the initial planted ideas of our limitations into firm roadblocks to our future success.

Once we stop blaming the person who implanted the idea of our limitations, we will be ready to begin rewiring brain's connections.

Life provides more opportunities to impact you negatively rather than positively, just by the way society works. So, to clean out and reform your belief system requires a constant awareness and clarity about how you want your life to be, and understanding and overcoming what is stopping you from reaching your potential.

CHAPTER 12

BACK TO WORK
AND GROWTH

I finished my doctoral degree and returned to my old job, my intent being to stay until I could figure out what I wanted to do next.

Going back to work after two years of sabbatical leave was very difficult. I had been under stress for so long a period that anyone had only to look at me for a second and I would 'stress out' to the point of bursting out crying. Through my experience with another 'grandpa', my advisor in the doctorate program, I had lost my capacity to manage and resolve tasks with ease, and without stressing out.

My recovery took some time and a lot of self-care. Eventually I was able to fully understand and appreciate that my nightmare was over and, despite the psychic pain of the process, I had finally achieved my doctoral degree.

When I got back to my job, while I was the same person I was before going back to school, I soon sensed a difference in the way I was being treated by my co-workers. Although I was saying the same sort of things I said before I got my PhD, now everyone was listening and agreeing with my opinions even when, in the past, they wouldn't have.

What I learned from returning to work to a different reaction, is that if you have a PhD after your name you are more noticeable. Some people think you know more and are wiser, which may not be the case, the addition of the PhD alters their perception of you.

I realized that because of others now perceiving me to be wiser, I should take more care with my opinions. Too much of what I said was being taken as the truth, without examination, and not just as a simple opinion.

Teaching

My desire to teach at the university intensified after I completed the PhD, but I could still hear in my head the voice of my doctoral supervisor telling me I did not belong there, that I lacked the skills and language proficiency to teach at a university level.

It was hard to silence those thoughts, but I am glad I didn't. Those words gave me the courage to prove him wrong, and I decided to apply to teach early entry courses, just to see if I could do it.

I have found that my varied life experiences allowed me to learn to strategize, and double strategize! Finding ways to overcome both my limitations and my fears has proved a challenge, but has also enriched my journey in life.

This time, my biggest fear was that my students would 'confirm' that past opinion of my doctoral advisor that I didn't belong there. I knew psychology well, and accepted the reality that I had a language barrier.

As English is my second language, even when I felt proficient in the language I feared that my students would equate my having an accent and average language skills with a lack of knowledge in the subjects I was teaching. With the advantage of hindsight, I think the barrier, fear related to my once pronounced language difficulties, was in my head. By the time I was teaching university students, I had no reason to believe I was still struggling with the English language.

Nonetheless, sometimes thoughts can have bigger effects than reality, so I needed to address my fears directly and find the best way to shut them down.

To assure myself as much as my students, I not only prepared very well the substantive material for my classes but also carefully prepared my "introduction'" to my students. I had a group of about thirty young minds in my first class. I began my first lecture by asking them if anyone of them was here, in my class, to learn English. After several confusing looks shared around the room, elbow bumping and short chattering moments between students, the response was that they understood the class was about psychology and that is what they were here for, not to learn English.

I replied by saying they were right, psychology was the topic of the course, not English. I advised that since English is my second language, I couldn't teach it, and admitted that I needed to improve my English.

So, at the onset of my relationship with my students I declared my weakness and validated my strength, which was and is psychology. I stated that if their intention was to learn about psychology, I was the right person to teach it. I related my experience in the field and how I was going to pass my knowledge on to them, so that they could become proficient in Psychology. I also asked them to help me with my English, so I could become more proficient in the language with their help.

This simple introduction took me out of the fear place in my brain and positioned myself in a place where the exchange of knowledge takes place, rather than in a place of weakness and power differentials.

Over the years, I have learned that allowing people to be who they are and coming into *their presence* without pre-judgment, and opening up to them as to what you can offer and what you cannot, allows your brain to be in a fully receptive, fully functioning mode. It also allows others to become totally receptive to interaction with you.

When the power differential between people is made 'not a factor' in the relationship, everyone involved becomes capable of bringing their 'best' into that relationship.

Good relationships are not about trying to establish power differentials between those involved but one of more or less embracing the differences, allowing both parties to enter into a win-win interchange, where strengths and needs can find a place of fulfillment.

Our Group, Sharing and Strategizing

Creating effective life strategies and sharing successes were the main intent of a group created in the midst of my worst experience, my pursuit of a doctorate. After school was done, my friend Deanna and I continued with the group of women, and we were all gaining ground in our lives with the support of and for each other.

Every second week, we got together to discuss what was working and what help we needed to get to move further forward. In my personal journey, I was debating between what I wanted to do and what I was doing in my work. I wanted 'more', but I did not know what that more would look like. Although I had a very rewarding job, with great worker-colleagues around me, I still wanted something else, though that something else was not, then, clear.

In my quest for answers, I found information on a seminar to be held in Santa Barbara California. The seminar was to be out on by Jack Canfield, the author of Chicken Soup for the Soul. I decided to attend. It was a good decision!

What I learned there not only allowed me to clarify my life purpose but also gave me some of the tools I needed to move forward.

During and from the seminar I learned that if I could make sense of my life now, which I could, I should be able to make sense of my earlier life.

I found myself looking back in time and thinking of my struggles, fears and disappointments. I realized that many of my past problems could have been less hard on me if SOMEBODY had lent me a hand. Why were and are so few supports for helping the young to grow up and become an adult? Why do we do 'that' (meanness, withholding help, failure to explain, etc.) to each other?

Life is a journey not a destination, and to enjoy the 'traveling', we should help each other.

That week with Jack Canfield was an eye opener for me. One session was particularly enlightening for me, it was about discerning life's purpose. Following a guided visualization exercise towards imagining our own life's purpose, I was able to visualize a Cornucopia[3].

I could see it very clearly, though I didn't have a name for it (in either English or Spanish). I was very confused with my vision. I didn't know where the vision 'had come from', or what was its cause? My vision was very clear, but also very puzzling. My first thought was that I was not doing the exercise right but had drifted away into my imagination.

After the exercise, we were directed to discuss our experience with a partner. I was sitting right beside an older man, later on I

---

[3]   A horn of Plenty

discovered he was a priest. He explained to me the meaning of the cornucopia, horn of plenty. He suggested that I think about a talent I had in abundance, one that would 'overflow from the horn'. I was even more confused; at first, I couldn't imagine myself as being represented as a horn of plenty.

Maybe I needed to find a horn of plenty! Well, it was good that we were asked to meditate on the horn of plenty, and to think about the meaning of our visualization. We were told that with time we would be able to understand its purpose. I left it at that, thinking: *Well I bet I did the exercise wrong . . . .*

When I returned home from the training, the visual image of a Horn of Plenty stuck in my mind, constantly. I kept trying to figure out the meaning of my visualization. I related the experience to our group of women and we looked up the dictionary definition of the Horn of Plenty, noting there a picture representation of it. We discussed various possibilities as to the meaning of my visualization, but, as it was my vision, I felt I had to understand it.

I sensed understanding my vision would lead me to find the real meaning of my life.

After four months of still wrestling with my initial experience with visualization (the Horn of Plenty), I began to conceptualize the idea of *'plenty'* in my life. What did I have that could be described as 'plenty'? I had had many life experiences, right from the onset of my life.

Somehow, I knew I had the ability to analyze and dissect those life experiences, and through that process discover the 'learning' that I should discover and which lay behind them.

I developed neurological explanations for my significant experiences, and I concluded that I could convert them into teachings and, from that, form varied strategies for life through which others, by adopting them, could save themselves 'the long road' of self-discovery and take a short cut towards enjoying their journey in life sooner rather than later.

I began to envision a venue, an approach, by which I would be able to transfer my concepts of successful life significant strategies to others in a coherent and meaningful way. Every night, I slept with a paper and a pen beside my bed. I was flooded with ideas while sleeping. My best ideas came in the middle of the night, and if I did not capture them then and there, by the time the day came the ideas would be gone.

I brought my ideas to our group every week. Even when they could not see the 'end product' as clearly as I saw it, they were all 'on board', ready to initiate the journey with me.

In my vision, I would teach women what I have learned in my own life journey, including how I was able to work through the many hardships I endured. I also wanted others to understand that we are not alone, but need to search for help to find and implement what we feel is missing in our lives.

Waiting for something to happen versus acting to make it happen is definitely not the way to go through and enjoy life.

I did not understand then what I know now. Everything I experienced, my adversities, my fears, my pains and my discoveries, were all part of a process. I was being trained, not just by formal education but also by my experiences, to do something 'bigger' than what I had done and achieved so far in my life.

I needed to wait to see where the process was taking me, and, at the end, how it was going to help me to find and implement my purpose in life.

On one hand, I had finally 'seen' the shape of where I wanted to go with my career, and I had a group of women ready to 'fly with me' and with my ideas for this new adventure, no questions asked!

On the other hand, I lacked the venue, money and human resources to implement my ideas.

I came to the decision that if I didn't act on my Horn of Plenty vision, my life would continue in a more or less predictable fashion, and excitement and accomplishments would be traded off for a more pedestrian journey.

Another important lesson I learned in from the seminar with Jack Canfield, was to never give up on something that you want. You should search relentlessly for the 'yes' that is hidden amongst the many 'no's' that are in the world. Most of our dreams are crushed with the first NO. If we do not believe that our dreams and ideas are important, or, even worse, we think we are not important, we will settle down to life with the NO's in command.

CHAPTER 13

SEARCHING FOR YES!

With my vision from the Horn of Plenty developed, I was ready to begin looking for my 'yes'. Timing was not an issue, I did not care how long it would take, I just knew in my heart that it was going to happen, and I had the rest of my life to make it happen!!

What was clear to me at this point in my journey was that I had to make things happen rather than wait for life to either give it to me or have it fall into my lap. Timing, location, circumstances, and the views and concerns of other people should not change your decision as to what you want to make of your life.

Nobody should wait for life, events or other people to tell them what to do. We are all capable of creating our own purpose in life, and when we find it we need to take care of the logistics required to make it happen.

I created a plan as to how my message would be delivered, and the kind of venues that would be appropriate. I also developed the information that needed to be available, concluded as to attendee attributes (the kind of people who would best benefit from attending), and devised how to invite participants.

I planned for regular sessions, and projected the costs as well as the potential and expected revenue outcomes. I concluded we could finance the events on our own.

When I had the seminar outline in my head, and had developed the full 'game plan', I began to look for an organization with an interest in similar matters. My seminars were initially designed to address what is required to produce "Empowerment for Women".

I felt closer to women as my 'target' attendees because I knew in my heart that I was not alone in experiencing hardships, I expected that many women had have experiences similar or comparable to mine.

I was beginning to understand the concept of *fulfilling your wishes* by having both a clear picture and feelings associated with desired outcomes. What I learned is that when you are emotionally engaged with your ideas, your ideas will drive you until they become a reality.

It is only a matter of time and patience. Later on in my development of seminars for women, the concepts I pursued were reinforced through my readings of the teachings of Wayne Dyer and Joe Dispenza

In the process of looking for financing and marketing support to sponsor my ideas, I asked twenty-eight organizations with mandates to support women. Every day I would target one or two of the agencies and present to them my ideas about possible venues, topics, and audiences.

I introduced my group of helpers and explained how we were planning to finance the events. We needed an organization that would agree to both advertise the seminars and assist with managing the finances. Our plan involved financing the events through contributions by private donors in return for tax deductible receipts.

I quickly learned to mention my professional credentials in asking for a meeting.

If I forgot to say *"I am Dr. Irene Estay"* before asking for a meeting, the answer was always,100%, no. The route to take in seeking a meeting with an organization's CEO or President included mentioning my academic credentials.

I found there was a great difference to the likelihood of success between the introductions "I am Irene Estay" and "I am Dr. Irene Estay".

Getting my first 'yes' was far from easy. I searched for my first YES for four months, every week I visited one or two agencies explaining my idea. Their 'no' responses, as to why they couldn't do it, were both very interesting and varied. Looking back now, I better understand why, as individuals, we become so 'boxed in' and limited that we don't think enough about the possibilities of doing good and succeeding.

I, myself, was 'boxed in' for many years. It was only now that I was starting to wander out of my box with confidence, taking some chances without worrying (about either what people did or would think about me, or as to what I could offer).

Some of the 'no' answers I received were:

> "We *don't know you; our board is not into those things; I don't think it will work; we have a plan and we don't deviate from it; we can't see the need for that; we don't have volunteers in our program; you can't work here, we don't have a position to fit you in; that is a high risk topic; we have never done that; we don't work with anyone that is not an employee; you will not get enough people interested; something like that will never work; and, we can't receive money for what you want to do."*

An official of one of the 'no' agencies even asked me how I was planning to dress for the event! I was never able to figure out what motivated her to ask that question; in my often-seeming endless search for my YES I always dressed professionally and conservatively for meetings.

The only thing we absolutely needed to have to be able to put on a seminar was an organization willing to receive donations, give tax deductible receipts, and invest in the materials and supplies needed to conduct the seminars.

I searched and searched for an agency willing to hear the idea, show some interest, and be capable to make a decision "out of the box".

YES!

The funny part of my lengthy search and journey for a 'yes' was the way the YES showed up. I was not prepared for it.

I had made an appointment with the agency's CEO, just as I had done with a succession of CEOs or presidents each day for four months to that date.

When I arrived for the meeting, I found a young woman in an office with piles of files and documents all over her desk and floors. It was a very sunny and welcoming office.

She was on the phone when I arrived, so I had to wait a few minutes until she finished her call. I began my speech just as I had done twenty seven previous times. She appeared to be paying attention, neither interrupting me nor even asking questions. Then her phone rang, again.

She gestured me with an open hand to wait. While I was waiting, I was planned my approach for the twenty-ninth agency, recalling my schedule to ensure I would have the time (I was working full time and, also, teaching one course at the university). It was the end of November, and I knew that December would not be a good time for my search.

I expected to continue my search in the New Year.

I had zoned out in my head and was not listening to her conversation, when, suddenly, she said "I will do it". I continued lost in my head until I heard a second "I will do it". Then, I thought she was answering a question or agreeing to a request of the person she was talking to on her phone. Accordingly, I did not give much thought about her "I will do it", and went back to my silent planning of my next appointment.

She then tapped her desk, basically demanding my attention, and again said "I am doing it".

In my confusion over her "yes", I didn't know what to feel.

Fear? Excitement? Anxiety? All those feelings were rushing in my body, the search for my YES had come to the end. I did not know what to feel; all I knew was that my determination to find a YES after so many NOs had finally yielded what I had always wanted, and expected.

She hanged up her phone, leaned forward and said: *"Tell me what I need to do, and I am doing it!"*

When she asked that question, "what do I need to do", momentarily I forgot what to say. I had to compose myself, and quickly recall just what I did need her agency to do. After a few seconds, I remembered that, at the minimum, all we only needed from the agency was for it to receive donations and issue tax receipts. We would solicit donations and make the arrangements for the venue, materials needed, format, etc. Her agency would be the financial administrator for my first Empowerment Seminar.

After we finished our meeting, with her having agreed to be a partner, I told her that I would get back to her with more details. My mind was racing at one hundred miles per hour, I could no longer sit still. My feelings were confusing. I wanted to transform my ideas into action, but now that I had the opportunity to do, I began to worry that, maybe, I could not do it. My old tapes of doubts and fears were ready to play in my head

My old negativity tapes were running wild: ideas of *"you can't, that is beyond you; your English isn't good enough; you are a little woman"*; and, *"you do not belong". These* thoughts that were running through mind were seemingly out of control, but, thankfully, only for a few seconds.

I had regained control over my thoughts, then I began to transfer the concepts that I had been developing in my head into concrete action steps. Now, my thoughts slowed down. I was well prepared, and not just in my head but also in my writing. Now, I just needed to take action.

The first thing I did was to call my friend Deanna. She would, and did, locate and deliver my good news of, at last, a 'yes' to every woman in our group. The second thing I did was to calm myself down, and begin to create and implement the real event, our first empowerment seminar.

As it was the end of November, and with December not usually a good time to invite people for a seminar (an Empowerment Seminar), particularly one to be presented by someone they did not know of, I decided to plan for the New Year.

Our group held an emergency meeting the very same afternoon I got my YES, and we began to work out the details of the seminar. Where we are going to get the advance money?, what place will serve as the venue?, and, How do we find the participants, the attendees, in such a short time?

Money was our first concern. Unanimously, we agreed to tap into our personal resources: husbands, other family members, friends, bosses, dentists and doctors were to be called upon. We needed enough cash to pay for the venue, the food and the needed materials. Fundraising by the 'yes' agency would be expected to raise enough to, at least, recover all our costs (although the recovery would follow not be ahead of the event).

We first discussed holding our inaugural seminar early in the New Year, leaving December open as a possibility. We had to have enough time to figure it out all necessary details. We were all so excited, we felt we couldn't wait another minute.

While no one in our group, other than me, could have known what exactly was in my head as to the substance of the seminar, nevertheless everyone was on board with the idea of holding empowerment seminars. They all knew that everyone would have a part to play in the process.

Another lesson that I had learned by then was not to wait for other people to come to you, even when you feel down or troubled. Build your support now, regardless of how you feel. Don't wait around for things to get done but pursue your objectives. If you have a need, whether it be advice, solace or specific help with something, go ahead and face your challenges, do what you need to do, call on people and take things on head on.

Look for what you want, and ask for your YES. Once you have created the support you need, rely on it. Most importantly, take full responsibility for your ups and downs during the process of realizing your dreams.

CHAPTER 14

SEMINAR NUMBER ONE

At our group meeting, and after much discussion, we decided, after all and despite the extremely short timeline, to hold our first seminar in December; only a few weeks away. We didn't think we could wait another month to see the first results of our idea in action. We only had three weeks to prepare for our first "Nurturing Your-self" seminar.

To start with, we had agreed on a name for the seminar, which was needed to advertise the event.

Our search for a venue began immediately, and we quickly found a hotel that had received a cancellation for the first week of December. We were fortunate, there was nothing else available anywhere in the city for a Saturday in December.

Talk about synchronicity, a December cancellation for a central Calgary, Alberta hotel. What were the chances of that?

We booked the place, having decided that if enough money wasn't donated through the efforts of our first sponsor, our first YES, we would still hold the event and split the cost within our group. As it turned out, the donation money did come in, although not until after the seminar.

I am pleased to report that since we started putting on seminars, now fourteen years ago, we have never been short of funds. As a result, the empowerment seminars continue to be held, and are financially self-supporting.

It was hectic times for the three weeks we had now fourteen years ago to 'launch' the first seminar. We were 'pushed' to get everything in place, But we succeeded. Of greatest importance was our need to have a sufficient number of participants, attendees. We approached the agencies I had previously approached fir support and asked them to send participants. As well we invited our friends. As the seminar was 'free' for the participants, donations were and still do support the events, this worked to our advantage in attracting participants.

Similar to the 'no' results I had encountered in my first visit to the agencies I sought grants and donations from, some of those same agencies didn't want "to risk" sending participants to an event that they had not, yet, agreed to support.

Our host agency, the first YES, did act, making a call for participants to the women they were supporting.

So, at long last our first Nurturing Yourself seminar was held, on December 10th 1998 the seminar was attended by twenty participants.

I learned in the process of arranging, funding and holding the first event in three weeks how to take charge, the importance of dreaming, the need to work hard to fulfill a dream, and the necessity of stopping at nothing to meet tight deadlines. From first visualizing the idea, then moving forward with it, to the first event's successful completion, I realized that at the end of the day, the only "expert" on your life is you!

My idea to hold empowerment seminars to help women realize their capacities and move towards their goals first arose from a visualization exercise that had prompted me to think about my purpose in life. And, out of this came the start of the seminars, although it took many months to transform my 'dreams' into reality.

When my idea had become a reality I was first stunned, amazed by the power we each have to create our lives rather than abiding by the tendency to coast along, allowing what other people say or do kill our creative spirit.

The first seminar was an awesome experience, not only for me but also for the group of women that trusted me and freely gave their support even before knowing all of my plans. The women that attended that first seminar provided great reviews of the it, not only validating my plans but also my purpose, that being to help other women first visualize their own preferred futures and then act on those visions.

I was able to use my own life experiences as a learning template for others.

The CEO of the first agency to provide me the opportunity to fulfill my purpose also attended the first seminar. She considered it her responsibility to do so as she took responsibility for supporting the event, not only the financial support through her donors but also for the participants she recruited for the event. She wanted to reassure herself that she had done the right thing. She was impressed and relieved.

Immediately after the successful launch of the seminars, we began preparing for the next seminar. We invited women living in shelters and receiving support from counselors, and physicians, friends and acquaintances referred others.

As I mentioned before, we have not ceased putting on the empowerment seminars since that first session held now over fourteen years ago in December 1998. Our relationship with the first agency to sponsor a seminar lasted but a short time. The CEO was pressured by her board of directors to insist on exercising control over the conduct and presentation of the seminars. Her agency's Board also requested that we form and involve "professional supervisors", to screen the women participating in the seminars. Since we intended to keep the seminars as a learning forum, we saw no need for involving outside professionals in the selection of participants.

By the time we were 'separating' from the first agency that supported our seminars, we had de-eloped an amazing and trusting relationship with another agency, one that was creative, visionary and willing to take us 'on board'.

Our work has not only continued with that then-new agency, Calgary Family Services, but led to the creation of a forum that has facilitated an expansion of the original concept. Our relationship with the agency is based on trust, respect and most importantly, and within a culture of creative out-of-the-box thinking, support for the members of the Calgary community.

Within the first year of the seminars, Deanna and I began to look for support in the community to continue providing the Empowerment Seminars at no cost for participants. We joined *Lions Club of Calgary* which accepted the challenge. The Club has been our strongest support since the onset of the Seminars.

Our seminars are now available for not only women, but also other groups of individuals, including teenagers, pregnant women, the elderly and men. The seminars provide a supportive, trusting and nurturing environment for us, as well as for the participants attending the seminars.

CHAPTER 15

A NEW CHAPTER
IN MY LIFE

After having created and developed "Nurturing Yourself Seminars", I discovered that the more I taught, the more strength I had in my own life and the more creative I was becoming in finding solutions for life problems.

I had taken on a great responsibility, that of creating life strategies for others, particularly women.

The seminars became popular, we have a full roster of participants every month and no longer need to search for participants. Past participants were coming again and bringing their friends, moms and daughters. Always, the feedback from participants has been that they want more, they want to continue in their journeys of empowerment.

So, shortly after the first year we created a second level of seminar, this for participants that had attended an initial seminar.

In the second level seminar, we provide participants more 'tools' to advance their own empowerment, while, at the same time, we encourage changes in their lives to reflect their 'new' minds.

We named the second level: Lessons Learned.

As noted, Lessons Learned was created for women that had attended the initial seminar and wanted to continue further in their personal journey. Observing women as a woman attending Lessons Learned, I was surprised to see how much of the information they had received from the level one seminar had been retained and employed already, and positively, impacting their lives.

Also, I learned how my own life experiences, as reflected in strategies I developed and share in the seminars, have been able to help other women begin their own journey, by identifying and removing the 'road blocks' to progress that they encountered.

By the second year of presenting the monthly empowering seminars, in addition to having a husband, two very active young adults and two dogs!, I was also working full time and teaching at the university, the latter on a part time basis.

I began to feel overloaded, and came to understand that my life was becoming unbalanced. My ethical question to myself was: how can I teach women to balance their lives and face their road blocks, when I am not doing it for myself?

At that point, I knew that something had to give, so as to re-create balance in my life. My full-time job brought a good income and excellent benefits for our family. As well, by then I was teaching more advanced courses at the university. (I had already removed the road blocks that had been affecting my teaching, so I was enjoying the rewards of teaching, which include the progress of my students.) I was also very much involved with the seminars.

It was time to review my workload and determine what changes were necessary.

A significant lesson I learned then was that it was important for me to recognize my creative ability as well as my ability to act on my ideas. Too often, we don't give sufficient attention to our thoughts, especially when they are negative (such as: I am never going to succeed; I am so dumb that nothing will work out for me; I can't do it; I am not good at it; English is my second language; etc.). We need to pay attention to our thoughts, and act to rid ourselves of negative thoughts.

Set positive statements in your mind, ones that will allow you to create exactly what you want to create, nothing less. And, after creating a "picture" in your mind of your ideal action(s), don't dwell on the 'how' for a while. Your mind will allow you to find 'the how' in time.

I share a quote from Mahatma Gandhi that speaks about 'your' thoughts. I found it inspirational from the start, but, until I created the seminars, it never occurred to me that the content was so true:

> *"Your beliefs become your thoughts, Your*
> *thoughts become your words.*

Your words become your actions, Your
actions become your habits

Your habits become your values, Your
values become your destiny."

As I heard other women's experiences, over time I became fascinated with the similarities of challenges that life has in store for us. What struck me most was the need of those women to share their experiences with others, and their often silent yearning for somebody to support them in their journey.

CHAPTER 16

CASE STUDIES

Over the now fourteen years of presenting the seminars, I have observed some amazing transformations in the lives of participants. These transformations began with their adopting new ways of thinking.

Providing yourself with the time required to explore your feelings, memories, obstacles and opportunities will allow you to move forward. You should move forward with the formation of a new idea of yourself, and as that idea gets connected with your feelings "you become" that new person.

Settled in your new persona, you will never go back to the past you.

My recounting of the experiences of some of the past seminar participants[4] allows me to illustrate the movement from thinking

---

[4] The names of the participants have been changed to protect their confidentiality.

differently to acting on new thoughts, and becoming a new, happier and more confident person.

Sharmila

Sharmila was a young Muslim woman that came to our seminar dressed in her traditional attire, with her head covered by a hijab. The first time she came to the seminar she sat at the back of a room filled with about 50 participants. I noticed her because she cried through the full day of the seminar. While I didn't have time to approach her that day, I could see she was quite distressed. Afterwards, while I wondered what was wrong in her life, I didn't find out until she showed up again at our seminar, about a year later.

This time, while her dress was similar to before her attitude was different. I could see her displaying a big smile, and noted that she had brought a friend with her, an older woman. And, instead of seating at the back of the room, this time she sat in the front row with her friend.

Minutes before the seminar started, she approached me and said she wanted to talk to me at the break. We agreed to connect right after the first break. She wanted to tell me what she had learned the first time she attended the seminar. At every seminar, I tell the participants that they probably came to receive one particular 'lesson', one that could change their life. She wanted to relate to me what that lesson was for her.

At the break, she provided me with personal information action about herself. Referred by her doctor, she came to the first seminar at one of the lowest point in her life. She had just come out of the psychiatric unit where she had been hospitalized for a month following her attempt to take her life. She was a mother of two, one girl of ten years old, the boy, only five. She then related the following story:

When *she was a little girl her mother told her she was the Daughter of Satan and whoever came into her life would also become part of Satan. She never questioned her mother's statement, believing it to be the truth. She never shared this belief with anyone. She made the decision that when she married she would never touch the skin of the people she loved the most—to reducing the risk of passing her 'condition' to them.*

Previous to attending the first seminar, she received a call from her son's school to let her know that her son was uncontrollable. The teacher said that "he was a little devil", kicking and biting the other children and the teachers. She panicked as she realized that she had not been careful enough with her son, and had touched him, and now he had become Satan. The incident brought on feelings of depression, anxiety and panic, so, for her, the only way she could help her son was to disappear. Thus, she attempted to end her life.

One of the lessons she got from attending the first seminar was the importance of touch: how our entire body is wired with touch sensors, leading to the importance of a nurturing touch for growth and development. She said that when she heard that information, she froze, not initially believing what she was hearing. But, she debated in her mind about her being Satan and being responsible for passing that awful burden on to her son by touch. When she returned home, she was more restless and needed to find out for sure what the truth was.

She got up that night and went to her son's room and began to caress him through the covers. She was too scared to touch his skin. She did the same with her daughter. Then, she began to get up every night to do it, and continued to do so until she felt more comfortable. As time passed, she began caressing her children's arms and faces, and as she didn't see any drastic changes in them during the day, she figured she was doing something right. Within a few months, she was giving full hugs to her children and she was enjoying their responses.

One day, she received a phone call from her son's teacher reporting that her son was doing amazing, participating in all activities while ending his previous biting and kicking episodes. She was extremely happy by the news, and decided she needed to do her "final experiment" (to see if touching her children had brought positive changes rather than she had passed on the Satan spirit).

She decided "to test her son". When her little boy returned from school that afternoon, he came running to her just as he had been doing over the past few months, wanting a hug. She pretended she was busy and told him to go and watch TV. The little guy came back a couple of times to her asking if she needed something, he wanted to help. Again, she redirected him to the TV and told him that supper would be ready soon and she would be calling him when she was ready. The little boy came back for the third time and said to Sharmila: "mommy could I have a hug even when I don't have to do any chores?"

Sharmila then felt as if a weight had been lifted off her shoulders, she enjoyed a happiness that she could not describe. That same night, she talked to her husband and finally told him why she had tried to commit suicide. They talked for hours before deciding that while they would continue visiting her mother they would never again allow her mother to influence their children in a negative way. As well, Sharmila began to look for a loving and nurturing older woman that could serve as a surrogate grandmother for her children.

She approached her neighbour, an older woman that had lived alone since her own children had grown up and moved to different parts of the country, and asked her if she could be a "grandmother" for her children, the neighbour agreed. With that agreement in place, they both decided to attend our seminar, a second time for Sharmila, to listen firsthand to the lesson that had saved Sharmila's life.

At the end of our conversation, Sharmila said: "I know I am a good person, so I don't need to worry about loving and touching my family anymore."

What I learned from Sharmila's experience was that the frontiers of our differences disappear when we become honest about our feelings and share our journey with others. Sharmila was able to cross cultural boundaries and openly approach someone she thought would provide the additional loving and nurturing attention she wanted for her children. She also found a friend and companion, someone that was lonely, missing her own children and ready to give more love to others.

If Sharmila would have kept herself within the boundaries of her culture she would never have had the courage to approach her neighbour with her request. It had taken her many years to understand and address the damage her mother's words had done.

Miranda

Miranda came into my life when she was just turning eighteen. My oldest son was travelling and trying to find his way when he met Miranda in Costa Rica. They became a couple and Miranda came to live with him in Canada.

Miranda was a fighter, life with her was like living in a war-zone. She felt she needed to defend herself from everyone and everything. While in Costa Rica, she was living with her grandparents, her mother was a single parent when she was born. When her mother later married, Miranda continued to live with her grandparents. As she described herself, she was a very difficult child and teenager.

Miranda was a bright and defiant woman, determined to push everyone away regardless of the consequences. She didn't trust anyone, and before she could get hurt she made sure that she pushed others away first. After being married to my son for a year, her relationship with him was over. Then, she found herself in a country with neither relatives nor friends, that is, except me. She had severed all of her other relationships, since she thought she couldn't trust anyone.

Despite the opinions of my family, I made the decision to be part of her life and became her *Floridena*. I sensed her heart was soft, although she was hurting herself all the time with her combative personality. It was less painful for her to push people away than to risk others rejecting her.

I remember the first time I tried to give her a hug, she responded with a cold attitude and stated that *it was not something that she felt comfortable with.* It took me a long time for her to soften up to a physical nurturing approach. Despite her attempts over the years to drive me away, we still have a healthy relationship.

Miranda has struggled most of her life, but now she understands that she does not have to live in the 'war-zone'. Life for her can be whatever she wants it to be if she is willing to be open to others and learns to understand that the world is not out to hurt her.

She is on her personal journey, one that includes attempts to overcome her childhood experiences of rejection and to heal the wounds created by others when she was a child. We all can do this if we are willing to look at our experiences from a different perspective, and find a *Floridena* along the way.

The changes that have occurred to her views as to her life are reflected in this letter, written to me, Christmas 2012.

Dear mom,

As I was thinking about a Christmas present for you, this print came to mind [two women embracing each other] . . . It reminded me of what you represent to me: a loving, caring individual who always has chosen to be there for me . . . Someone who has comforted me and taught me how to love unconditionally (still working on it!) but none the less to love in a way I never thought I could . . . I love you mom and I hope you know how grateful I am to you for always loving me and being there for me . . . I hope we can continue spending many years together . . . . Love you. Miranda

What I learned from Miranda is that love can conquer any negative experience, but you have to be prepared to weather the storm regardless how hard and long it can be! When a person lacked positive and loving experiences in the most important years of their life, as a young baby, it takes longer to learn the positive lessons of life. If you have somebody to help you along your way, you may get to understand how life should be, even after missing those important early lessons.

Miranda has become an amazing woman, a supportive sister for her stepsisters and a great daughter for me. She has embraced her experience and since understanding what her journey in life should and can be, she is present, loving and nurturing to her two younger step siblings. Now, she is also a complete wife and future mother, with a partner willing to love her unconditionally and help in her journey. Now, she ready to pass on her legacy to her first child.

Suzanne

Suzanne was a very strong and intelligent woman, very successful in her job. She was an executive of a large organization, making decisions and managing one hundred employees. That was at work; at home she had a totally different reality.

She was the mother of two young adults, a fourteen year old son and a seventeen year old daughter. She was devastated when her daughter announced that she wanted to live independently, was planning in finding a job and would quit school. Suzanne came from a very traditional family. In her culture, the understanding is that a girl should live at home until a gentleman asks her parents for their daughter's hand in marriage, this before they can enter into a relationship.

Suzanne was a very protective mother, and she had plans for her daughter. It never occurred to her that her daughter wouldn't comply with her plans. This new reality threw Suzanne into a severe depression, which included feelings of incompetency as a mother. She blamed herself for being a working mother, not home to teach values to her children. This message was reinforced every time she had a conversation with her mother or her sister; they reminded her of the traditional role assigned by their culture to women and mothers.

She attended the seminar, and learned about *Affirmations* as a way of keeping herself focused on what she wanted in life, rather than on what she didn't want. Concentrating and thinking of what is wrong in our lives and what we don't want only brings more of what is wrong and what we don't want.

Maintaining in your mind a picture of what is not presently in your life only creates more of what you don't want rather than leaving the space reserved for what you want, your own ideal. To find solutions to our problems and to bring into being what we want, we have to be clear in our minds what we want.

Comprehending that her view of what her daughter should do was so much in conflict with the position of her daughter that she, Suzanne, was having difficulty even listening to her daughter, Suzanne created the simple affirmation: *I am happy and content, supporting my daughter's decisions.* With this Affirmation in her mind, Suzanne set out to listen to her daughter, towards gaining a better perspective on her daughter's thinking.

Nonetheless, an affirmation such as Suzanne's created structural tension in her mind. The tension arose because her affirmation was false, not true. Her 'verbalization' was of a feeling that wasn't actually true in fact the opposite to what the reality actually was. Suzanne was not *happy and content, supporting (her) daughter's decisions.* Suzanne was stressed, worried about her daughter leaving home at such a young age, and before completing high school. Every time Suzanne tried to converse or have a discussion with her daughter, Suzanne's fears would become stronger, and she would feel scared, sad and challenged.

Suzanne would then argue with her daughter about her daughter's poor decisions, 'telling' her that she was throwing her life into the garbage. Suzanne hoped her daughter would understand her, particularly given Suzanne's, own childhood experience of having few resources as she grew up. She failed to realize that her daughter wasn't having the same experiences, her daughter's material needs were being met, and abundantly.

Armed with her affirmation, repeating it on a daily basis, false as it was, helped Suzanne to *listen* to her daughter when her daughter did want to talk. When, as her daughter spoke about her plans, Suzanne began to feel stress and fear overwhelming her, Suzanne would concentrate on her affirmation in an attempt to align her feelings such that she would be able to listen.

Suzanne understood that her belief system (regarding life, needs and family culture) were driving her fears. She also understood that her daughter's experiences and learning where just that, her own, and if she wanted to understand her daughter she needed to abandon her own belief system and look at her daughter's needs in a different light, one from the perspective if her daughter.

The affirmation became the signal she needed every time she began a conversation with her daughter, and began to feel anxious and fearful. Eventually, with the help of many talks with her daughter and Suzanne struggling to remain objective and listen, she was able to align her affirmation with a true feeling of happiness with her daughter's plans. And, after a few months, Suzanne helped her daughter move out on her own and find employment.

Since she was supporting her daughter's decision with the help of her affirmation, she was open to listen to her daughter and, gradually, both of them came to actually understanding each other's differences, challenges, views and decisions.

And, later, with time and circumstances changing, Suzanne's daughter went back to school and graduated from University, with the support of her family.

The relationship between mother and daughter changed, and they developed an open, nurturing relationship that was not judged for what it should or could have been but more for what it was, real for them as individuals with different life experiences.

What I learned from that experience is that we are unique.

Even when we share many experiences, the way we process the information creates different sets of belief systems. By developing our *listening skills,* we are better able to understand the other person beliefs, particularly if we accept that they can be different. We can create a relationship that is supportive, respectful and allows for individuality.

On a personal note, I can relate to Suzanne's experience with her daughter. When my sister and I discuss situations and events from our past, she remembers the experiences of our childhood totally differently than I do. We were both there, but for each of us the significance of the events was based on the way we processed the information at that time.

Maria

Maria was a woman in her late fifty that attended a Spanish speaking version of our seminar. She was also a member of a support group for Spanish speaking participants. She was from El Salvador and had entered Canada through the assistance of Amnesty International[5].

---

[5]   Amnesty International is a global movement of more than 3 million supporters, members and activists in over 150 countries and territories who campaign to end grave abuses of human rights.

Every year since we started the seminars, we hold a social function for participants that have joined "support groups" to continue with their personal growth. The women get together to celebrate their accomplishments, individual and group. Participants are encouraged to write a statement on a card to describe their individual accomplishments for the year as well as the support they received from group members.

For our Spanish speaking participants we have volunteers that translate their statements into English for the benefit of the overall group. We got to know Maria after she wrote on her card: *"Since I started with the group I don't think about killing myself every day . . . I know that every couple of weeks other women are counting on my presence."*

When the volunteer translated her statement, the room, which was full of people, became totally silent. Nobody knew what to do or say. Tears flowed from other group members as they were looking at Maria while she was sitting at her table oblivious of effect of the translation. The silence seemed forever until a person seated beside Maria stood up and hugged her, and then everyone else began to move towards her to do the same.

Maria's husband and her two young sons were killed by guerrillas[6]. Her family had been approached for money by the guerrillas and, since they didn't have any, her husband and children were murdered in front of her. She escaped to another city, and

---

[6] Guerrillas can be understood as groups of individuals that are against a traditional government and live in the mountains. To survive, they kidnap others and demand ransom money from civilians.

people there helped her connect with Amnesty International which brought her to Canada as a refugee.

At the age of fifty, she found herself with no family, in another country, and in a place where she could not understand the language. She met a woman that had participated in our Empowerment Seminars, and she brought Maria to the seminars.

Later, she became part of a Spanish speaking group.

Deanna

Deanna, a member of the women's group that launched the seminars, was in charge of the music played during the seminar's exercises. Despite being confined in a wheelchair and having limited upper body mobility, she brilliantly designed the wide variety of music played.

Why music? Well, music can be an ally in bringing forth long lost memories and re-locking revised memories. If you were to take a 'picture' of your brain while you listened to music, you would see your brain 'lighting up' like a Christmas tree.

The activity elicited by memories and music takes place in several parts of the brain. Recalling memories result in many bodily sensations which we interpret as feelings. Music aids in locking up, storing for retrieval, information by 'wiring' and connecting neurons located in different brain locations and in different patterns.

Our brains are 'plastic', and we can employ that characteristic to learn, unlearn and relearn, the memories, and the information we retain.

Deanna and I researched all types of music (quiet, inspirational, funny and upbeat music) as we matched up the various seminar exercises with the type of music that would elicit different kinds of emotions (reactions) in the participants. During the seminars, Deanna, sitting at the back of the room, would select the appropriate music, while following the presentation and participating in the exercises.

One of the exercises requires participants to create a picture in their minds as to what they would like to have in their lives. As for Deanna, her unrealized dream was expressed by a simple statement: "I *wish I could go back to school.*"

When she related her wish to me at the end of one seminar, I asked her why she didn't go back to school. She had made a list of the 'why nots' and as we reviewed the list we developed a set of options for each one of them. With financial limitations being the first on her the list, she realized that her set of reasons (beliefs) for not going back to school were, while numerous, all addressable if she was willing to challenge and revise her belief system

She had been fiercely independent all of her life. She wouldn't let anybody do anything for her, that is until she became fully dependent on other people for many of her day to day physical activities. Her body was the first one to challenge her independency-based belief system.

Despite her physical limitations, her business was editing and typing documents, resumes and other various papers for others. For the past twenty years, and from her home, she had helped many professionals, as well as university students pursuing and gaining their degrees, with her amazing knowledge of writing styles, formats, and the requirements for thesis and dissertations. She had a list of clients that, starting out with her as students, had become successful professionals. Most of her student clients kept in touch with her over the years.

After reviewing her list of beliefs that were preventing her from pursuing her dream, returning to school, she, through the exercise, began to challenge each and every one of them. As a start, and to address her financial restriction, she decided to write a letter to her long list of past clients and friends, to share what she wanted to do, her plan to return to school, and ask for their thoughts as how she could manage it.

It is difficult to challenge core beliefs, and independence, financial independence was one of them. So, after she mailed her letters, she felt sick, ridden by guilt. However, it was not long before she began to receive external feedback on her 'return to school' plans from her letters. Responses flowed in from family, former clients and other people she had shared her hopes with. Overwhelmingly they exhibited a different set of beliefs than Deanna's with respect to independency versus interdependency.

In less than a week, letters of emotional and financial support were overflowing Deanna's mailbox. The letters validated the useful contributions she had made to the lives of her past customers and friends, and family; the recipients of her letters expressed the joy they were experiencing from having an opportunity to contribute back to her, by helping her achieve her goals.

Revisiting long-held belief systems, beliefs stopping you from moving forward, is one of the most important steps in the process of self-empowering. We often create road blocks for the achievement of our goals, and rarely attempt to even question them.

What I learned from Deanna's experience, and from those of many other participants, is that self-limiting beliefs are strong impediments to overcome. Unless we challenge them head on, they will run, and could ruin, our lives. And, we may never realize that self-limiting beliefs were our worst enemy when it came to our being able to open up our opportunities.

First, we need to remove the barriers to progress that lie in our head.

Sofia

Sofia didn't wait too long to begin creating changes in her life, after attending her first seminar. She attended a seminar on a Saturday, and within two weeks of that day she had devised a *plan* for changing her life for the better.

After having divorced her husband of fifteen years, for the past two years she had been so depressed, anxious and very stressed that she had been unable to function in many areas of her life.

She had two daughters and shared custody of them with her ex-husband. As a result, she saw him on a regular basis at her girls' functions at school and at their sports events. Before attending one of her daughters' soccer games or school meetings, knowing she would encounter her ex, she would suffer stomach aches, vomiting, neck stiffness and all kind of other negative physical symptoms. She expected arguments with him, and that the encounter would distress her.

After two years of this then ongoing mental anguish, she was exhausted and ready for a change.

The plan that Sofia created was very simple, she began to visualize herself protected from the negative feelings and behaviors that had created her feelings of stress whenever she was in any form of contact with her ex-husband. She also decided not to engage in any arguments or discussions with him, whenever and where ever she had to see him.

Her plan was simple. When in the presence of her ex, she would begin to reinforce herself, by thinking about all her positive qualities and how she would view herself if she was displaying those qualities to others, especially when she was in the presence of her ex-husband.

The first opportunity to try out her plan arose at a baseball game involving her younger daughter. In the past, she always arrived late so she could sit as far away as she could from her ex. This time, she waited in her car until her ex reached the bleachers and then proceeded to sit right beside him. In her head she repeated to herself and visualized all of her positive qualities, even when she was experiencing the physiological effects of fear and stress: heart pounding, hands sweating, stomach cramps and head spinning.

She greeted him with a casual 'Hi', to which he did not reply. She then concentrated on the game as much as she could. At the end of the game, she said goodbye, receiving no response from her ex. The new approach and resultant experience boosted her confidence and she decided to maintain her changed behavior until the signs of stress and fear were gone forever, thus meeting her objective, the main goal of her plan.

In upcoming weeks, she repeated the same routine. In one opportunity, and to her surprise, he answered her 'Hi and Goodbye'. As the weeks advanced, she became braver. And, at one point, she told her ex-husband a story, and without any strenuous effort or animosity they began conversing about the game and their girls.

For the first time in two years they were talking without animosity or argument. And, she was actually feeling at peace with herself. Just changing her mind, aligning her behavior to her new idea and forcing her feelings to align with her "new mind" and her "new behaviors" had worked, even after having been involved in a dysfunctional pattern for more than two years!

There was another issue, since the divorce Sofia had cut off all relationships with her ex-husband's family, who she missed terribly since she had had a very close relationship with her sister-in-law. As her plan was to find peace for herself, and create more nurturing relationships in her life, she kept on thinking about her ex sister-in-law.

The test of her courage soon came; she stood at her sister-in-law's door ringing the doorbell. She said that the minute the door opened her first instinct was to run. But, when she saw the surprised look on the face of her ex sister-in-law and the tears that were in her eyes, she thought about the time that she had wasted feeling resentment and anger. Some of that anger had been directed at a person she cared for, one that had nothing to do with her relationship with her ex.

It took Sofia two years "to change her mind" and to begin to create different outcomes in her life. Her learning began with her decision to *create the better life she visualized for herself*.

Amanda

Amada came to the seminar at one of the lowest points of her depression. She had been attending therapy for a year, yet she felt she was not able to move further ahead through that process.

Amanda was in her early sixties, living with her daughter and taking care of her two granddaughters. Her daughter had been diagnosed with *Dysthymia*, a chronic depression with the longer and lasting symptoms than comes with a major Depressive Disorder. Amanda felt she was not only unable to help her daughter but that her granddaughters were more than she could handle.

As always, at the beginning of a seminar I tell the participants that they may learn one or two lessons in the process and, if they are willing to implement those lessons in their lives, their lives will move in the direction that they truly want. In the case of Amanda, the seminar exercise focused on *finding purpose* was the one that created a positive change in her outlook and behaviors.

Up to that point, she had never thought that her living with her daughter and taking care of her granddaughters had a very specific purpose (as she explained later).

With the seminar exercise she was able to *"change her mind"* from seeing herself as a victim, a woman trapped due to circumstances, to an individual not only responsible for the wellbeing of her granddaughters but also one serving as the critical support to her daughter (allowing her to work on her image of herself, so she too could get better).

By changing her mind, she changed her attitude towards her situation, and that eventually changed her feelings from ones of sadness and depression towards feelings of hope and optimism. She realized that by becoming a more optimistic person she had become a role model. By displaying her attitudes, outlooks and skills to her daughter and grandchildren, she created a shift in their views and skills at the same time.

When she came back to her second seminar about six months later, she told the participants that she was no longer depressed and that she was working every day to create the behaviors that would sustain not only her wellbeing but the wellbeing of her family as well.

What I learned from Amanda's experience was the power of awareness.

Once she became aware how she was contributing to her own mental state of feeling hopeless, and came to understand the importance of her state of mind, she was able to change her mind which, in turn, led to positive changes in her attitudes and feelings.

My final case study that I report is the case of Esther, a distressed young woman who seriously considered suicide. To allow further appreciation of Esther's case, I recount it in the first person as Esther described her story. To distinguish her accounts from my comments, Esther' s report is presented in italics

Esther Decides to Die!!

It was 2 PM on a Saturday afternoon, I was in my apartment in the 9th floor facing 6th Ave downtown Calgary. I was standing in front of the window that access the balcony. I was feeling out of control looking around and moving frantically in the apartment. I was observing the kitchen cabinets with all the elaborate design in the doors, the pictures on the wall, the ornaments that I had that reminded me of Colombia. The furniture was covered in brown material and I was bouncing my attention from looking through the windows and the brightness of the day and my furniture and belongings inside. I was in that state for sometimes. I had the letter that I received from my family that day in my hands that said how much they loved me and how they were missing me.

I was thinking over and over how they would suffer when they knew about my decision. I could no longer bear my life. I was living a nightmare for so long that I did not had the strength to continue. I had no hopes, nor any desire to continue being alive. I was unable to find happiness in anything. That terrible experience had left me naked, alone, emotionally destroyed with no desire for living. My awareness was shattered and my thoughts at this point were incoherent.

I had turned myself into a paranoid woman. I was afraid of everyone, I was thinking that everyone had a double life and most were horrible people. I was afraid all the time and I was thinking that at any time somebody would kill me. I was working and going to school and I had to pretend I was OK but my fear was a constant companion and I could not work or pay attention to what I was doing.

Every time I would get home I would close my doors and check them many time before hiding under the bed . . . waiting for the assassin. At the most during the day or night I would change spots and I would go to hide in the closet under many layers of bedding so if the assassin came, he may not find me and I would be spare for one more day.

As I was standing in front of the window, I was thinking about my mother. Her suffering and despair when she was told about me. Then I thought, maybe I should write a letter to my family, friends so I can explain why. Especially my mother, I could visualize her grieve. "I am so sorry mom" . . . the phrase kept on coming to my mind, over and over . . . I could not think anything else. My decision was taken. I needed to take care of the details. The idea of peace, of never thinking about my experience, of never being scare again anymore was more attractive than what my family would suffer.

I had made my decision. I could not take it anymore, as I was writing the letter, the idea of peace was more attractive than my mother's pain. I was embracing myself, caressing my face, my head while tears were filling my eyes non-stop. Kept repeating to myself . . . it will be over soon . . . you will be okay Esther, it will be over soon . . .

I had a mix of feelings, on one side I wanted to continue living but on the other side I was thinking that I had lost my soul. I did not have a soul.

I went back into my past remembering the day that I was walking the streets in Canada with a smile in my face. I was happy, I was ready to start a new life in a country of opportunities. I have goals, projects, the love of my family and friends in Colombia, the desire to begin a new life. That day, when somebody took my soul, everything was over. I tried to remember when I began to experience the fear, when the treats began, the physical punishment, the mental anguish when I began to do anything to be alive. It was hard to remember, it was like I went into a depth abyss and I didn't remember when I fell, when I lost my soul and I knew in my heart, that I could not get out alive.

I began to tremble and cried with more intensity and saying to myself . . . is not fair . . . . Esther . . . You cannot die . . . . It is not fair . . . . On the other hand a voice was telling . . . now do it! It will be over soon . . . do it . . . now it is time . . .

While in that internal debate I ran to the phone and called my friend that lived a few blocks from my apartment building and I screamed and pleaded to her . . . You need to be here now! I need your help! I don't want to live and I don't want to do something crazy!! . . . Please! Now . . . DO IT NOW!!!!The urgency for me to do it was there . . . Esther . . . . do it now before your friend get here and it will be over soon . . . you are crazy . . . you have to do it now . . . Do it!!

They were only a few minutes of constant struggle until I heard the phone ring . . . it was my friend calling me to open the apartment door. When she arrived to my apartment I held onto her sobbing.

The next thing I remember is when I opened my eyes . . . I was in my bed and my friend was beside me, looking at me with big eyes with a panic on her face. I think she never stopped looking while I was sleeping, her face showed a great deal of worry about me. With a loving voice she whispered to me . . . . My girl you cannot die yet . . . you have a long traveling to do still . . . .

Literally I felt as I was buried alive. It was as if I had fallen in a very profound and dark hole with many levels. Every time I thought I had touched bottom, the earth would crumble under my feet and I would fall again another under ground level. Again and again, getting out was almost impossible at this point . . . I wanted to get out and have a normal life. At times when I could relax, when the fear was away for a couple of seconds, I was making plans of having a normal life and the next minute everything would go back to the way it was. Panic would set in and I would continue in my nightmare. I felt as I was pretending to have a normal life and at times I was not sure if I had imagine what I was remembering and it was not real. I was really crazy.

A gift from God

After all the suffering, I received a gift from God. It was the phone number of a Psychologist that spoke Spanish. I was very happy. I had the sense that this will change my life forever. I thought she would understand me.

In my first encounter with Dr. Estay and Calgary Family Services, my heart was racing very fast. I tried to relax but the more I tried the harder it was. At the bottom of my heart I was ashamed that she would find out that I was becoming crazy. I tried to sound and look normal since I knew as a Psychologist she would know right away that I was crazy. I scanned her office very careful for cameras since I wanted to make sure that nobody was spying, and that the person that wanted to assassinate me would not come there to fulfill his mission.

My first visit with Dr. Estay was totally different than other Psychologists that I have seen before. She appeared to be interested in me, trying to understand me, and she was speaking my language! So I did not need to worry about her understanding me.

To begin with, the lack of communication was resolved. We were speaking about my problems. This was a real counselling session and not a workshop in English proficiency which in the past left me exhausted and unable to explain my feelings. I did not have to translate something as profound as my fear in another language that may be nobody would understand. With other professionals I would spend the hour trying to translate my experience with a broken English without being able to express the depth of my fears.

This Psychologist was patient. She did not sent me to a Psychiatrist or talk to me about antidepressants. She was listening intensely and was explaining what was happening to my body from the perspective or science and psychology.

I was telling her about my repetitive dream. I was a small child, about five years old lost in an immense and dark forest. I was crying for my parents, I wanted to find them in the forest. I wanted to go back where I left them before. In my dream everything was dark with trees that did not let me see around. The trees were organized in circle and I saw myself standing in the middle, raining, dark, and scary. I was crying and extending my arms to the sky so my parents could see me and they would come to rescue me. I knew that the wolves would come soon and would viciously devour my body piece by piece until was nothing left.

My dream would always stop when the wolves were coming closer and closer and one of them would jump towards me. I would be exhausted and petrified with the dream every single time.

I loved the Tuesdays. That was the day of my therapy. On that day I was a normal person. The psychologist would assure me that I was not crazy and that we would work together until I was totally ok on my own.

I knew that she did not judge me. I could ask any questions and I was not afraid to be rejected as I felt many times when I wanted to share my fears. From Wednesday to Monday I would become tormented with my fears again. On Tuesday morning I would cry since I knew I had to organize my mind and go over the experience so I can re structure my thoughts with her. My therapy was hard. I had to confront my fear, myself and my trauma.

Every Tuesday when I left her office I would go straight home to be by myself. I did not want to see or talk to anybody so I could process our session. Every week I felt as I was shedding of my tormented mind. Every night I would thanks to God for the opportunity to heal and to be able to understand what was going on in my mind. The light was coming into the depth hole little by little. Now I had hope that one day I will be completely out.

When I attended later the Nurture Your-self Seminars I understood the fear as a condition in my body that I had control over. I also learn that I could control me, my depression, my self-esteem even the paranoia. I was not crazy. My psychologist explained to me that I was suffering from a Post-Traumatic Stress Disorder (PTSD) and both of us were working to defeat the enemy! I could not wait for the sessions since we united in forced against the enemy!

Through the teaching I understood that the enemy was no longer the person that took me hostage, threatened me and physically abused me over and over until taken my soul. The enemy now was the trauma that he had created in my mind and I had allowed him to be present in my life every day since the first day for over a full year!!

I understood that I was the only one that I could defeat and destroy my enemy. Without being fully aware over the course of my therapy, I was getting enough tools enough to conquer my paranoia that had settled inside me.

It was a matter of time and work for me to be fully healed. I was yearning to live a normal life and every time I would work harder with by beliefs, my mind, my body and my spirit. I had the tools to do it!

It was like a hand pulled me out of the hole that I was in for some time. Finally I was seen the light. It was no longer darkness around me. I remember the dreams of the little girl lost in the forest. When I dreamt later about the forest, I could see the trees, the sun, and the color of spring. I could smell the air and touch the water. I was no longer scared and helpless lost in the forest. I could see the trail that was taking me where I got lost from my parents in the first place.

Everything was left behind. I was now left with the experience, the courage, the strength and a profound feeling of thanking God and the persons that came up to pull me out of the hole. I could feel the love of my family and the strength of that love to push me towards my future.

Now I feel that everything is behind me. I am left with an experience. I am ready to dust the dirt of my clothes, healing my wounds and take my luggage that I lost when I was walking the streets of Calgary where I lost my happiness, hopes, professional goals, the love of my family and the illusion to begin a new phase in my life in a land of opportunities.

I am grateful to God since he never left me and has always put in my way what I need to enjoy my journey . . .

Recovering From Post-Traumatic Stress Disorder

What Esther describes in her account is labelled in psychology, *Post Traumatic Stress Disorder.* The memories and or the external stimuli takes over and the person is in total fear mode at all times.

All environmental stimuli or memory flashes trigger the fear and the panic response. The person has given the control to the body and the mind to respond to the events that created the initial panic response. The "self" is completely out of the picture. The self was interpreted by Esther has her connection to a higher power-GOD, as her ability to control her mind and body as she describes it. The process for Esther was to regain the connection with "the self "and develop the strategies to manage her mind and body.

In our last sessions she stated that she was *testing herself* all the time to see if the fear or the paranoia (as she called it) was still there. She would purposely place knives at the kitchen counter at home or walk very close to a man. Both stimuli would have triggered the panic response in the past. When she is calm and no physical and or emotional reaction appears, she still think that it is strange . . . and she tries a next time.

Now is time for Esther to trust that she has regain the "power of the self" and what is left in her memories are only memories with no emotional charge and the presence of loving and nurturing connections with her family and friends that allowed to stop her suicidal attempt at 2 PM on a Saturday afternoon in her apartment in the 9th floor facing 6th Ave downtown Calgary.

My Perspective

During and over the now fourteen years I have been working with women through the seminars, the lessons learned for me have been endless. The process of bringing about positive change regularly achieves our goal for the seminars.

Positive change in the attitudes and actions of our participants happen in so many ways. And every story we hear, arising out of or in our exercises and discussions at our seminars, when our participants feel connected, can be a trigger for someone, a trigger for them to create a new set of positive behaviors, discarding the old negative feelings and behaviors.

Change involves letting past and present negative feelings and people 'go'. Change involves a decision to discard the pressure of a long-term memory that has been disrupting one's balance in their life.

Being able to see these processes working for others, and to be able to validate my contribution to them, is one of the greatest source of satisfaction arising out of my work. I value the reality of positive changes that have been created, and I value the amazing and growing group of collaborators in bringing life to processes that help people live fuller and more aware lives.

Participants in the seminars get together in small groups and help each other in finding new and improved ways to better enjoy their lives. They also recognize and employ ways to help each other, and others outside of the seminar environment, with their issues.

The presence and growth of *peer support* over the past fourteen years has helped me to understand the need that we all have for each other in enhancing and completing our journey in life. Each one of us can be a *Floridena* for someone else. Your contribution to that person will have a positive impact for the rest of their life journeys.

When you decide "to change your mind", you will positively affect the way you feel about things, and that will motivate you to change your behaviors. Changing your mind for the better is a process. If you consider how many people you will come in contact with over the span of your life and how you could impact their lives, it becomes apparent that the effort is well worth it.

Roll up your sleeves and begin the journey to a balanced life, and don't worry, you have the rest of your life to complete the work!

CHAPTER 17

PLASTIC BRAINS

We have 'practiced' all our lives to-date to do what we do and be who we are. As Miguel Ruiz[7] says: "We *are the master of our personality, our beliefs, and every action and reaction.*"

In order to change what is not working for us, we first have to be honest with ourselves. We need to become aware when we are not doing what we should be doing to realize our potential. Research suggests that 99 % of our actions reflect habitual behaviors, and that we pay little attention to either our imagination or to creating new behavioral patterns.

Once we are honest with ourselves and understand the responsibility that we each have to ourselves, we then need to accept ourselves and others as we and they are and begin to 'work' on ourselves. It is important that you become and act in accordance with what you are, not what other people think you are or should do.

---

[7]   Miguel Ruiz.(1999)The Mastery of Love.

Only when you find your own truth will you be able to find your balance and begin the life journey best suited for you, discarding negativity along the way.

I have worked with a wide array of individuals, developing activities and exercises to assist them to increase their personal awareness, so as to allow them to find their own fulfilling journey in life. In this chapter, I outline activities that have proven effective to 'unwire' and 'rewire' the neurons of countless seminar participants, towards creating better personal outcomes. To enter in a new awareness of yourself and then change your way of being, requires that you change your mind. Changing your mind involves entering into the space where *habitual behaviors* reside, the actions we do every day without thinking what we are doing.

We cannot change something we are not aware of. Accordingly, achieving personal awareness is the first step for changing. Personal awareness requires understanding your behaviors and, emotions and realizing when they are not in alignment with your purpose in life.

We live emotionally, and we can gauge our state and healthiness of our lives from the way we feel. If we are not happy, at peace, content and hopeful most of the time, we need to find and review the reasons why we have allowed our lives to be out of balance, and begin the change.

Responding to life becomes automatic and habitual, once we learn certain patters of behaviors we no longer question them but use them every day, and many times. Only when we "wake up" can we realize that we are not enjoying life anymore.

Learning to live happy, useful and contented lives follows the same principle of any learning. Initially we must become very aware of our reactions, after that we can learn to respond differently, consistent with awareness.

An example of this process is driving. When you were learning how to drive, all of the proper behaviors had to be *present.* The knowledge of traffic lights, rules and regulations, the existence of only two feet and three pedals (assuming a standard transmission), checking your rear-view mirror, not killing anyone crossing the street, turning at the right time, etc. I could go on and on, but you understand the process of such learning.

Now, after a few years of driving, none of those required behaviors are "present" in your mind. Your driving becomes more or less automatic. While driving, you are thinking about the grocery list, laundry that you need to do, the friend that you are going to meet, etcetera.

Learning *who you are* exactly follows the same pattern as when you learn to drive.

You may have been four years old when you heard your dad saying *"hey, you are a bad brother, you should share your toys with your baby brother"*. When you heard that criticism, you might have internalized it, but altered the thought from the specific to the general, now it is not just your action that you perceive to be bad, but you, yourself. At the same time, you likely interpreted the tone used by your father as being not pleasant, and could have extended that observation to your father 'overall'.

Bad begins to be your interpretation every time your dad either reacts with anger or is upset with you. Over time the tittle of *being bad* takes a life of its own and you start to translate it into other areas of your young life.

This process, initiated initially by one person, in one particular situation, begins a fixture of your belief system that gets reinforced over and over again; until you no longer question that you are bad. It has become your internal representation of who you are.

Now, move on to other important figures later in your life. The past words and actions of coaches, teachers, relatives, and other people that you trust begin to paint a picture of yourself that you internalize. Why would you not believe them? It is natural to take their opinion of you as a truth, since they are the people you trust they must know who actually you are! But, do a few words spoken by them about you a long time ago and in a specific situation really represent you? Likely not!

Those seemingly innocent encounters over your life are the ones that created who you are. You don't question the veracity of every one of those statements, and some of them become part of your definition of yourself.

If you want to change the statements that had defined you up until today, you have to bring them to your awareness and start to rewire your brain to construct the "new you", through the same way the initial statements you need to delete entered your mind.

The good news is that the brain is plastic.

We can make up changes to how we think of ourselves and others. It will take time to create the new neuronal connections. But, once they become part of your revised memory, those neuronal connections will take on the strength of the initial dysfunctional statements, since the new rewired brain will need the chemicals previously used to maintain the false interpretations to maintain the new circuit.

If you are to begin your own process of finding your way to a more healthy and balanced life, you need to change your mind's interpretation of yourself, change your behaviors and change your feelings. That is the path to understand and know the proper and healthy significance of your life.

It sounds a big job, but it is not. You only need to understand the importance of doing it and begin your journey. There are no time lines; you have the rest of your life to do it. So if you do one exercise per month, the exercises you will find further into this book, in a year you will have advanced in twelve new directions, and you will have embraced a *new you* in twelve different ways!

Getting rid of your old and negative habits will take time and determination. While doing so is not 'rocket science', you need to think how important it is to live your life to the fullest. This is the only life that you have, and you are entitled to live it to its best!

And, even if you 'came back', if that was possible, you would not remember this life. So, you might as well do what is necessary to enjoy this one! Towards gaining control of your life and realizing your opportunities and potential, and as I do in our seminars, I now ask you to work through a series of 'assignments'.

There need be no rush, take your time. I assure you that through the diligent completion of the assignments, however long it takes you to complete all of them, your 'plastic' brain will change and you will be better for it.

CHAPTER 18

FINAL THOUGHTS

I have learned that we are all 'a work in progress'.

We would best never stop learning and growing, especially about our potential to become a better person. This process of making ongoing efforts to improve every day, until the day we depart this arena that is life, should be a central focus of our lives. We all need to improve our ability to understand and enjoy life more, and we need to stop 'sweating the small stuff'.

There are many 'Masters' we can learn from, many who have done at least some of the thinking already and have created ideas on how to move forward and enjoy more of our journey.

Several assignments preceded by a self-agreement follow, and it may be best for you to undertaken only one lesson at a time until you have finished them all. There is no time clock, and no one should rush you. If you do work carefully, thoroughly and honestly through the assignments, I fully expect that, given time and allowance for regression from time to time, your life will become more enjoyable. And, as you work through the assignments, you will feel different and begin to question why you are not having much fun with your life. You will start making 'adjustments'.

Some simple changes, such as simply becoming aware of 'traps', traps such as: paying too much attention to other people's needs and too little to your ken, will help. And, realizing that you are spending too much precious time focusing on memories and negative thoughts that are ruining your present moments will be a start. These and many other 'traps' have not been 'kind' to either you or those you care about.

And, we need to objectively observe and assess our relationships. If we can focus on and deliver on what can make us better persons, we will have a different and happier experience through our day to day journey.

Life can be good, but only if we allow ourselves to experience it that way. When we take on other people's agendas, our life becomes complicated and unfulfilled; no longer is it our life to enjoy.

When we are a child we have no choice other than take what our primary caregivers are able to provide for us. If they weren't very skilled, or were not present enough to fulfill our needs, or, worse still, abusive, we need to remind ourselves that it was not our choice to be there.

But, when we become adults we should 'own our own mind', completely, and choose how we want to experience our day to day existence in the now.

Over many years of life and professional practice, I have come to understand that if we work with our minds, come to understand the basic principles of learning and unlearning, and develop and maintain some basic values to guide these processes, we can, pretty much, create whatever life we want for ourselves.

Herein is the awareness and knowledge that has allowed me to carve out the life I wanted, although, it is very important to note, the process at arriving at this point took me some time. Even now, I don't pretend to be done with my 'carving', making changes to the way I think and do, all I know is that I will continue making changes as long as I can.

And when the times comes that I can no longer 'do it for myself', I hope I will have, by then, created a legacy of nurturing environments and loving relationships that will continue to be shared with and among others.

What follows is a summary of what I would consider the major 'take away' points to be gained by reading my book and completing the assignments, again, the assignments follow and are an integral part of the book and the messages contained in it.

Understanding your past, obtaining this level of understanding is not about making sense of your past as that would complicate your perception of the past even more. It is about understanding that the people that were responsible for you while you were growing up acted based on only the knowledge and understanding that they had of themselves at that time. If they had known better, most likely they would have done better.

In my life story, I was gradually able to understand Grandpa, appreciate Floridena and the many others that were kind to me, and accept the pain and sorrow of my mother who lost her partner far too early.

I made a decision on becoming an adult, to 'let go' resentments and abandon my 'should be's, 'could be's and 'was not''.' I have found that adopting 'forgiveness' to be one of the greatest strategies one can employ. If you want to enjoy the 'now' and life itself, **forgive**.

Understanding the plasticity of the brain is one of the keys to happiness. Our brain is like sculpturing dough that never dries! We can shape and form it the way we want, any many times over the course of our lives.

We would best come to understand that there is nothing—people, environments, our past, our memories included—that need keep us tied up forever. We do need to become aware of our patterns of behaviours and the actions that need to be changed or deleted. Memories only have the strength that we give them to interfere with our present.

Research indicates that we need three to four weeks to change behaviour. That is, if we keep that troublesome behaviour present in our awareness along with alternative approaches to replace it.

Becoming aware of your thoughts and emotions is critical.

We mostly live in our thoughts and by our emotions. As I earlier noted, we have about sixty thousand thoughts a day and another sixty thousands tomorrow and every day after. If we are not aware of the messages provided by those thoughts, we would best remind ourselves that they are affecting our emotional world on a second by second basis.

When we became aware of what we are saying to ourselves sixty thousand times a day, then we can begin to change by supporting ourselves and creating the conditions that we want, towards finding balance so we can begin to enjoy our journey.

When you come to paying attention to those thoughts, then you can begin to choose the messages that support you rather than those that keep you down.

The assignments that follow have helped me to move closer to the balance that I want have in life. They are both very simple and powerful, the power being in the opportunity to change your mind and begin living in the direction of your choice.

Experiencing positive emotions and dealing with negative ones is an important element in bringing about change. Understanding the dynamic of positive and negative emotions and how they affect our minds and body brings an amazing and useful element of knowledge that can, employed properly, contribute to our 'change' agenda.

CHAPTER 19

POST-SCRIPT

I close by further recommending the publications of Dr. Barbara Fredrickson[8], which should increase your awareness of research in this area. Her writings will assist you in your effort to achieve and maintain a well-balanced life, one replete with positive rather than negative emotions.

I hope that by relating my own experiences that led to my overcoming barriers and creating positive changes in my life will help you in finding your own path. I know from direct experience and observations that completing the assignments that follow have helped many other women and men in improving their life's journey.

The assignments, with their exercises, provide simple but powerful tools that can, if you undertake them seriously, shape your life to the way you want it.

---

[8]   B. Fredrickson (2009) Positivity

Every time you make a change in your life for the better, it creates a ripple effect that benefits others. And, when you share your gifts, both talents and positive emotions with others and become a 'traveler in life' that is enjoying her or his life experiences, you will make this earth a better place for all of us.

I wish you an adventurous undertaking of the assignments preceded by the self-agreement, and, please keep in mind there is no rush, contemplation followed by serious resolve and action takes time.

Namaste

Assignment 1: Your Self Confidence Agreement

As you begin your journey, you will quickly realize that one of your greatest enemies is your lack of self-confidence. To overcome this, you will have to use all of the resources available to you: positive thinking; visualizations; acting 'as if'; writing out, memorizing and repeating what you seek until your 'wants' become part of your brain cells and replaces the old and previous belief systems. Always remember the neuroplasticity of the brain when working on "changing your mind". If you make this agreement with yourself, rest assured that if you live up to it, and use constructively, it will work.

First Agreement. I know that I have the ability to achieve my purpose in life; therefore, I will be persistent, and I will take action toward this purpose.

Second Agreement. I understand that if I change my mind I will change my behaviors. As I think differently, I need to act in agreement with my new thoughts, first consciously until they become my new habits. I need to make a point to 'think' my *new thoughts,* daily.

Third Agreement. I know that any desire that I persistently hold in my mind will eventually seek expression through my behaviors employed to attain the object of mu desire; therefore, I will devote ten minutes daily to demanding of myself the development of self-confidence.

Fourth Agreement. I will clearly write down a description of my definite chief aim in life, and I will never stop trying until I develop sufficient self-confidence to attain it.

Fifth Agreement. I fully realize that my journey will also benefit others if I build my path on the principles of honesty, compassion, truth and justice. Therefore, I will not engage in behaviors or ways that will not benefit me and all whom I encounter. I will succeed by attracting to myself the forces I wish to use, and gain the cooperation of other people. I will sign my name to this agreement, commit it to memory, and repeat it aloud once a day, with the full faith that it will gradually influence my thoughts and actions so that I will become a self-reliant and successful person.

Signature   Date

Assignment 2: Who Am I? Rewiring my Brain

Over the course of our life to-date, we have received many messages that have guided our ways. A good number of them have been negative and limiting messages. This exercise is the beginning of your journey. Changing your descriptions of yourself should be the most important step in your validating process.

Create a list of qualities and characteristics that are the opposite of all the negative and limiting beliefs that you now hold about yourself. Once you have created the list, you need to begin the process of entering it into your memory, by daily practicing a ritual that involves informing yourself 'who you are'.

This process requires for you to utilize all the learning strategies that are available to you. These learning strategies are visual and auditory: looking at yourself in a mirror when repeating 'out loud' your list of qualities. Kinesthetic and tactile: write the descriptors you want to apply to you, and visualize what you would look like or what you would be doing if you had the characteristics you have written or said to yourself.

Use the statement **I AM** before each characteristic, it will become a command. Initially you will feel uncomfortable, even silly, as you will feel you are lying to yourself. In effect you are lying, that is until the characteristics no longer sound as they are lies, as they becomes a new neuronal connection in your brain and it becomes a part of you.

Remember, we are 96% habitual behaviors and any new behaviors will be questioned by your internal dialogue. When your internal dialogue is no longer questioning your statements, you will begin to align your new thoughts with the behaviors that represent your "new you".

Any negative statement/characteristic you say or feel will be made aware to you every time you are in misalignment with the new sought-after characteristic.

I am sick	I am well
I am a bad person	I am a good person
I am inconsiderate	I am considerate
I am a negative person	I am a positive person
I am resentful	I am grateful
I hate myself	I love myself
I am poor student	I am an excellent student
I am lazy	I am hard working

Assignment 3: Working your Negative Feelings

Negative feelings produce negative attitudes and negative moods, creating a state of being not conducive to our innate ability to be in balance and at peace. Our thoughts trigger neurotransmitters that affect the way we feel. And negative feelings 'kick' the desired homeostasis out of your mind and your body. To address negative feelings, you need to first address the source of those feeling and then change your mind about your control over such feelings.

There are two 'feelings' that are likely habitually present in your consciousness, they are feelings of resentment and guilt. Once you understand these feelings and responsibility for them, the emotional weight that they place on you will become lighter.

> Resentment: *I have a belief as to how people should be and they are not.*

When you become aware of your feelings of resentment, ask yourself the following question: Do I have the power to change others? The answer is no, and as part of the process I need to become responsible for my own feelings of resentment.

By taking 100% responsibility of your own outcomes, you will come to understand that the actions of other people are beyond your control, unless they, themselves, are willing to produce a change for themselves.

I resent _____ because I expect him/her
to _____ (be/do/have) as I (would be/do/
have) for myself.

I understand that I have no control over _____
for his/her choices in _____. I can only be
responsible for myself.

Guilt: *I have a belief of the way I should be that does not match my behavior*

Guilt is a misalignment between your beliefs and behaviours.

There are only two ways to deal effectively with feelings of guilt:

1. Change your belief to match your behaviour, or
2. Change your behaviour to match your belief.

Assignment 4: Changing my belief or changing my behaviors

Changing **my beliefs** that is making me feel guilty	Changing **the behaviors** that is making me feel guilty
I feel guilty when I have to leave my children alone when going to work	*I feel guilty when I have to leave my children alone when going to work*
Belief: Working mothers are not giving the children the time they require to become healthy adults	Belief: Working mothers are not giving the children the time they require to become healthy adults
Change: the quality of the time with the children is more important than the quantity. I will make sure to have quality time with my children after I get home. I will organize the weekends and my days-offs around them with purposeful activities.	Change: I will stop working and assume the financial responsibilities of the limited income.

I will be at home with my children while I think it will be beneficial for them |

When a situation arises that makes you feel guilty, choose the option you prefer to bring yourself back into balance. To bring about balance requires you to either challenge your belief or change your behavior. Once you find the option for you and act accordingly, you will eliminate the cognitive dissonance[9].

Repeat the exercise over time, so when you next think about the situation you will begin to rewire the new behavior or new belief (unlearning and relearning) until it becomes the way you now behave or the way of you now think. Either process will restore the internal feeling of balance.

You will be surprised to realize that there are many circumstances in the day to day live that we place ourselves in Cognitive Dissonance.

---

[9]   **Cognitive dissonance** is the feeling of discomfort when simultaneously holding two or more conflicting cognitions: ideas, beliefs, values or emotional reactions.

Assignment 5: Becoming Aware of my Incompleteness

Over time, you will have accumulated many experiences, and your view of many of them are not helping you move ahead, but, instead, clouds your vision to the present and prevents your creating a newer and better future. You become stuck in your habitual behaviors; you continue harbouring resentments, 'should dos', regrets, and 'must dos' but haven't yet.

If you are not aware that your MIND is full of wounds and emotional poison, it is because you have not been taking account of the emotional cost to you of that history. And, you can't begin to clean and heal your wounds and let the past go, and it is the past that is in the way of your present and a better future. If you want to struggle less in the rest of your life's journey, it is time to close out your resentments, and drop thoughts of the 'should dos', 'regrets' and 'must dos' but haven't.

The following exercise will help you bring your 'incompletes' to your awareness, and allow you to close or dispense of them by taking away the energy that keeps them alive.

Identify the following categories and write them down.

Broken Agreements	Unfulfilled Promises	Unfulfilled Wants and Needs
_____	_____	_____
_____	_____	_____
_____	_____	_____

```
_____        _____        _____
_____        _____        _____
_____        _____        _____
```

Once you create the list you should assign them to the following categories,

Complete **C** Renegotiate **R** Change time lines **CT** Replace for something else **RP**

Begin to work on each category; each and all of them are using up your emotional energy. They may not all appear to you to be important, but once you cross them of your list, you will find renewed energy and an enhanced desire to move forward in finding your path.

If there are many items on your list, make sure that you take the time and space to address each and every one of them. After all, you have the rest of your life to get them out of your awareness. It is best to make sure you deal with all of them within your own timelines. And, if you have a partner in this pursuit, create your timelines with your partner as doing so will make you more accountable to your timelines.

Assignment 6: Success is a Learned Behavior

As you let go your *wasted emotional energy* by acknowledging the events and circumstances that have been taking your energy, it is also time to refuel and learn to appreciate the part of your history that is composed of successes.

Now, while something you accomplished when you were a child may not have a particular significance to you right now, but remember that when you accomplished it, it brought with it positive feelings, new learning and the awareness of success. It created a cocktail of great chemicals in your brain, expressed through feelings of joy, exhilaration and excitement. Just think about what it meant for you to learn to ride a bike or to roller blade, or to win a school spelling contest.

As we get older we stop appreciating those past moments of successes and begin to concentrate on our failures. When you think about failures and negative experiences, your chemical body informs your brain and negative feelings such as depression, defeat and sadness arise, creating a downward spiral in your internal chemical balance.

On the other hand, if you begin to bring memories of success to your present awareness, your chemical body begins *to inform* your brain that we are moving to 'spiral up', and the chemicals associated with positive feelings begin to act in your body.

Divide your life into three stages: Early Years, Middle Years and Present.

Timelines (ages)	Events in my life	Lessons Learned
Early years		
Middle years		
Present years		

For each category, list your successes. There is something about writing things down that begins to move minds in the desired direction! And, as you write, begin to think about the lessons and opportunities that you are gaining from this 'new learning'.

Our mind responds to feelings associated with remembering. To create positive feelings, you need to think of situations that created positive feelings for you, and this will allow you to 'tap into' your internal motivation drive to create more of good memories in your life. Remember that feelings are associated with chemical changes in our bodies and we can trigger those changes by memory alone.

Assignment 7: Taking 100% Responsibility of One's Emotions

As individuals we live emotionally. Emotions tell us whether we are enjoying or hating our lives. Emotions are signals, alarm systems telling you how you feel about your life at a particular moment. Taking 100% responsibility for the way you feel means that you have to begin paying attention to your internal language and as to what you are doing now that is maintaining feelings you don't want.

Every day, you wake with a certain amount of mental, emotional and physical energy. If you allow your negative emotions to deplete your energy, you will have insufficient energy to change your life, let alone improve it or support others. Nobody can make you feel sad, mad, upset or even happy. In your use of language, you tend to give away your responsibility for emotions: *he makes me sad, she makes me upset.* Learning to take full responsibility for your emotions means you have to understand than no one but you can make you happy, sad or mad. If you listen to your emotions, you will begin to understand the changes you need to implement to create balance.

Create a list of activities that allow you to recharge and take full control of your emotions. These activities can be as simple as asking for a hug from somebody you love up or as complex as resolving critical issues that you have been ignoring for the longest time.

Things that I can use to recharge myself:

A foot massage, inviting a friend for coffee, a funny movie . . . .

_____

_____

_____

_____

_____

_____

_____

_____

_____

_____

_____

_____

_____

Every time you take charge of your emotions, you are taking charge of your internal balance that is translated in emotions.

Assignment 8: Facing Fears Head On

The first feeling that appears when you want to do something new, something that you have no point of reference of, is, too often, fear. Yet, many people when undertaking "the new" are starting exactly at the point of fear. Given this reality, we must conclude that fear is not the problem. Isn't?

One definition of FEAR is that fear is a **F**antasized **E**xperience **A**ppearing **R**eal. Fear takes a hold of your awareness, and fear is only in your head. Once you act on whatever is causing fear, you are addressing the fear, and it, the fear, is already behind you.

You can face fear in two ways, with a position of POWER, choice, energy and action, or, with a position of PAIN, helplessness, depression and paralysis.

If you have a fear of heights and don't want to jump from an airplane, that fear makes no difference in your life. But, if you fear success, that is a different story. Such a fear will affect your life in major ways. The secret in handling fear is to move from a position of pain to a position of power.

1. Become aware of the fears that are holding you in facing your life challenges
2. Identify in the chart below where you see yourself with that fear.

PAIN—I—I—I—I—I—I—I—I—I—I—I—I—I—I—I—I—I—I—I POWER

3. Go through each one of your fears and position yourself within the chart.
4. Pick one fear that have to move the least from pain to power and spend time deciding on the steps.
5. Begin the process with the situations that creates the list amount of fear to the most.
6. Stay with the experience until you can reach the position of power with your fear

Fantasizing about Fear.

This is an awareness exercise that
can begin to remove the fear.

Select one action, situation that is causing your fear.

Begin to imagine what it would be if the fear was bigger!

What would happen to you?

Use your awareness and reason to counteract that fear.

Example: You are afraid of spiders and imagine the spider is so big that it will take you into its web to eat you. By using your new awareness, you can create an internal discussion about the situation and conquer the fear.

Assignment 9: I am feeling stuck in my life

Sometimes, we get stuck in one aspect of our life, whether it be work, personal relationships, 'should do's' or unsatisfied personal goals. There is always a 'payoff' for being stuck. I need to say this twice, there is always a payoff for being stuck! There is something about being 'stuck' that is more comfortable or rewarding than moving on. Once you discover exactly what your payoff is, you can assess it and choose to take on the challenge of becoming 'unstuck'. If you think the effort will take too much out of you, so much that being 'stuck' is preferable, consider other aspects of your life where you are 'stuck', and begin to get 'unstuck' on at least one matter, instead of being led by fear or resistance to move on.

Exercise

1. In column one, list all the aspects of your life where you feel stuck.
2. Go back to each item in column one and write the pay offs in column two.
3. Where the benefits of being stuck are stronger than your desire to be unstuck, go on to another item, select one and develop a strategy to become unstuck with it.
4. Develop small steps and begin the work.

Areas of my life that I am stuck	What is the payoff from being stuck
- I am still smoking - I am being a victim - I am stuck in a job that I do not like	- I don't have to deal with the withdraws - Stop receiving sympathy from others. - I don't have to feel down by rejections while I look for another job

Assignment 10: Regaining your Power, Working with Day to Day Behaviors

Many times during the course of a day, you act automatically. And, you likely behave in ways that consistently reinforce your sense of low self-worth. Remember, approximately 96% of our behaviors are directed by the unconscious part of the brain, so we are usually in 'automatic mode'. The way to change negative behaviours is to bring them to your awareness right after the event, and consider the options for a response next time. Place yourself in an awareness state, rather than on automatic.

Every time you bring your behavior to your awareness, that behavior is no longer running your life. At that time, you can choose to 'keep it' or 'change it'; change it if isn't giving you the results you want.

Exercise: Discuss with a partner.

- Being aware of all the options you have for actions during the course of a day.
- When confronted with a difficult situation, consider all the possible ways you can act, and feel, about it before acting.
- Closing your eyes and picturing yourself as feeling happy, sad, outrageous, or humorous.
- Making the situation into a game, and "choosing" your behaviour/feeling for the "next time".

- Choosing a behaviour or feeling that will benefit you, even when you know it is going to be hard for you to act on it.
- The fact that the more you behaviours come to your awareness, the easier it becomes for you to wire a new way of approaching the situation the next time.

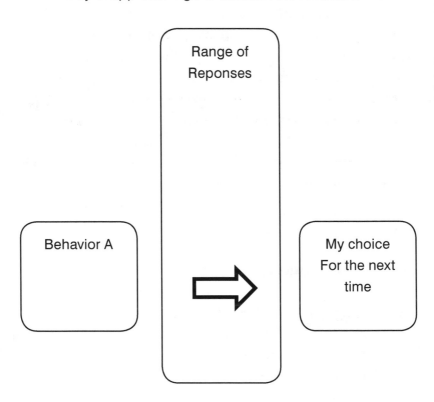

Assignment 11: Forgiveness is the Key to Healing

Forgiveness is the only way to heal your emotional wounds. We must forgive those we feel have wronged us, and not because they deserve to be forgiven but because of ourselves. We want to be able to love ourselves, as love helps 'cure' our minds of negativity. We don't want 'mind diseases' to run our mind. So, we should choose to forgive because we feel compassion for ourselves.

One of the first to forgive is you, ourselves. We all make mistakes that need to be forgiven. By forgiving yourself, you choose love over judgment. That's a good choice. You are also giving notice to yourself that you are moving on with your life, rather than remaining in the emotional prison of self-condemnation.

There is nothing you have done that cannot be forgiven, no matter how bad you think it is. We are so hard on ourselves and, sometimes, we set impossibly high moral standards. It is no wonder we suffer. Here's a five-step process to avoid this trap:

Step # 1 Forgiveness is compassion—Give up self-flagellation. There is no value in continuing to punish yourself, even though you feel you deserve it.

Step # 2 Accept what you did—Denial is a common way to get out of being responsible, and rationalization helps us disown responsibility. Take full responsibility for your action or inaction.

Step # 3 Confession—Is one of the oldest and best methods for unloading heavy burdens. It is a spiritual good to feel whole again. Confess to your higher power, to God and/or to someone else what you did. We share our humanness by showing each other that we, too, make mistakes.

Step # 4 Make Amends—Make amends if appropriate. A sincere verbal or written apology may be all that is required. Perhaps you need to return something, or pay back money that you owe. Have no expectations of the outcome. Be aware that sometimes the consequences of making amends include causing more damage, so think it through first. If is that the case, take the charge away from your awareness

Step # 5 What did you learn—Mistakes have a habit of reoccurring unless you acknowledge the mistake with your eyes wide open. All of life's experiences are designed to teach us something. Don't miss the significance in the lesson.

Learn to forgive yourself. Travel through life lightly, unburdened by guilt. It's one of the best gifts you can give yourself and those you love.

Assignment 12: Now, Begin to Forgive Yourself and Others

Once you have completed the process of forgiving yourself and dropping your feelings of guilt, shame, resentement, it is time to expand on the process of forgiving, and forgive others. There are very good reasons to complete this process. As you do it, you will find added energy for your days and the emerging of new and positive feelings toward others.

Four Great Reasons to Forgive

1. **To heal your body**—eliminate your toxic thoughts, including anger.
2. **To heal your heart**—let go thoughts of revenge, and feelings of ill-will, and begin to love unconditionally.
3. **To heal your relationships**—explore the potential for reconciliation or re-connection.
4. **To heal your life**—pain and resentment should not define you.

Exercise:

Begin the cleansing process. Write down any mistakes, failures, or things that you have done that you now need to be forgiven for. Include on the list the hurts and resentments you still hold towards others. This is for your eyes only, so don't hold back.

Whatever emotions accompany this exercise, experience them fully, for they are part of releasing negative feelings and allowing yourself to live in the positive feelings.

I choose to forgive myself (others) for:

_____

_____

_____

_____

_____

_____

_____

_____

_____

_____

_____

_____

[10]*"Your past cannot be changed but you can change tomorrow by the actions you take today."*

[10]   B. Fredrickson (2009). Positivity

Assignment 13: Unloading your Negative Past

We tend to carry so much negative baggage with us most of our lives and it just continuously weigths heavy on our shoulders. We need to clear the 'skeletons out of our closets', and unload the burdens of resentment, guilt and negative experiences that keep dragging us down.

Try the following exercises for a couple of weeks, and see how you begin to feel empowered and in control of your actions and outcomes.

Exercise 1

> Choose a situation that sometimes comes into your mind, one that you have decided it is time for you to let it go. Make an agreement with yourself as to how you are letting it go. Write down the action steps and check your agreement on a weekly basis to see how you are doing.

Exercise 2

> For one week, start writing down thoughts about negative experiences from your past and collect any of the following items that can trigger negative feelings from your past: old pictures, old gifts, letters, mementos, journals and keepsakes. Remember, when you are writing thoughts out and collecting items related to it, do it one at a

time so your mind does not get confused as to which negative experience you are letting go.

Once you have written down the experiences and collected the related items; make it a point to let them and the writing paper go: donate, recycle, burn, tear down, throw into the garbage. Tell yourself the reason why you are letting them go. Make sure that you complete the process and visualize that they do not longer are taking up 'space' in your mind. Do the process for any negative emotion you want to let go.

Exercise 3

Find yourself a big boulder or a rock, something heavy enough for you to notice when you carry it, and associate it with a negative thought or experience. Carry and keep the stone with you for one week.

Consider it like a pet rock, only this one is not very friendly. Take it everywhere with you (if you can manage to carry it in your pocket, do so all week long). After one week, if you are ready to let it go, take your rock and go to a place where you can throw your rock (example—a river or over a hill somewhere) away, and, with it, your negative past. You can either publicly express thoughts, feelings and emotions or silently do so as you are throwing the rock away.

Another suggestion is to take whatever glass bottles and jars you have and label each one with the name or feelings that have hurt you. Go to your nearest bottle recycling bins and recycle it.

Any exercise that allows you to travel lighter will have a great impact in your wellness and your emotional wellbeing.

Assignment 14: Closing Chapters

Over time we tend to accumulate thoughts and ideas, and we are always reminding ourselves of the things that we have not done, missed or failed to complete.

All those things have a weight in our awareness and keep us tied down to our 'incompletes'. Imagine that you have a limited space to keep information, and that those 'open chapters' of our previous life are taking up a great space. Getting rid of those 'incompletes' can free our minds, open up our perception to the new, and allow us to become excited with better and more interesting things to think about.

Closing chapters is about renegotiating in your head all your incompletes and negative memories, relieving us of negative energy that is holding on. Eliminating ideas that you are not planning to act on, closing out the "may be, when" and doing the things that are possible within reasonable timelines simply makes sense.

For some reason, writing down creates a stronger commitment to do something than just thinking about it. Go back into your memory and create a list of thoughts that are weighting down your mind, thinks such as:

- I resent my mother for not being there when I was a child.
- I didn't like my elementary school teacher who used to put me down all the time,

- I resented my classmates when they called me names,
- I was scared every time my boss approached me with a negative comment, and
- I missed having many friends, and thought something was wrong with me,

As you think about those situations, state to yourself that you are letting them go right at that moment. Check your feelings and make a check mark ☑ on the ones that you feel that is no longer bringing any negative emotions to your memory. Do it every week until your list is clear, and then begin another list until there is nothing heavy in your memory bank weighing you down from the past.

Assignment 15: Dealing with Obstacles

Obstacles are mostly in our heads. When we have an idea, we immediately begin to question the chance to make it a successful reality.

The 'ifs', 'maybes' and fears begin to crawl into our imagination. They are the most common response to a new idea. We create obstacles in our heads before we even begin to develop the idea. We automatically begin to think of what has not worked in the past, the number of times we have failed on other things, and, most importantly, what others are going to think about us.

The next time you stop yourself from exploring a new idea, or when you run into a roadblock, create three possible alternatives as to how to overcome your resistance or the roadblock, change your thinking or go around the roadblock.

There is a number of ways that an idea can work. The only way to find the way ahead is to brainstorm possibilities as a regular routine. By looking at alternatives and persevering, new ideas will come into your field of awareness, until you find the one that you're willing to try!

Alternative one

Alternative two

Alternative three

Alternatives of Choice.

Write down the steps to follow and the knowledge obtained from the experience.

Assignment 16: Increasing my Positive Feelings

Positive Psychology research studies have demonstrated the benefits of experiencing positive emotions, as well as the detrimental effects of experiencing negative emotions. Dr. Fredrickson has collected research papers from around the world validating these findings. In her book, Dr. Fredrickson illustrates six vital facts about positivity. It feels good, changes the way the mind works, transforms the future, puts a break on negativity, obeys a tipping point for changes to overflow all aspects of your life, and you can increase positivity by choice.

Finding positive meanings in your day to day existence is always possible. It is your choice to select the emotions you want to feel as the outcome of a particular event. Eliminating the negative is not the goal, the goal is to re-frame your mind to a healthier state, and where the chemicals giving you experience are not creating a negative effect on your body.

Creating a *positive frame of mind* and experiencing positive emotions can be your choice, even in the worst of circumstances. Look at the history of disasters in the world and you will see that not everyone had the same attitude as to those circumstances. Some people are devastated, and cannot see the way out; others seek an opportunity to create a new beginning after the event; and, others seek refuge in their belief in a higher power to overcome their devastation.

Positivity has identified ten forms of positive feelings that will alter your life and your brain chemistry to create a healthier emotional and psychological wellbeing: Joy, Gratitude, Serenity, Interest, Hope, Pride, Amusement, Inspiration, Awe and Love. Even while emotions are highly individualized, they have a common denominator; they increase the neurotransmitters that make you feel good.

Exercise: Create a list of activities or memories that brings you any of the below listed feelings. Consistently use the list to change your emotional state every time you are experiencing a negative state such as anger, anxiety, hopelessness or depression. The mind cannot differentiate between what is real and what you're asking your imagination to create. The neurochemistry of your brain will do the rest!

Joy	Gratitude
Serenity	Interest
Hope	Pride
Amusement	Inspiration
Awe	Love

Assignment 17: Creating your Treasure Box

Now that you understand the importance of positive feelings and your ability to choose them over the negative feelings, it is time to begin to create your treasure box. The way to wellbeing is to become aware of the things and memories that bring you positive feelings. Finding positive meaning is always possible, especially when you are aware of what you are trying to accomplish, that being a feeling of Joy, Gratitude, Serenity, Interest, Hope, Pride, Amusement, Inspiration, Awe and Love.

You may ask: Is that possible? Of course it is! Since we have the ability to manage the chemicals in our brain by managing and choosing the memories and events we want to remain in our lives. Finding positive meaning is always possible, but keep in mind, simply eliminating the negative is not the intention.

Exercise:

Find a box or a drawer in your home and identify it as your treasure box. Every time you think a positive thought, remember a positive experience or somebody that brought you joy. Get into the habit of writing a note and place it in the box. Memories or images that you have during the day, past holidays, pictures that make you smile, a song, a perfume; keep building your treasure box. As you get into the habit, you will create an ability to remember what you have in your treasure box, and it will bring the feelings associated with whatever you placed in your box.

As you become more creative, divide your selection to match the feelings associated with the positive emotions identified by Dr. Fredrickson.

- Gratitude
- Serenity
- Interest
- Inspiration
- Awe
- Love
- Hope
- Pride
- Joy

Assignment 18: Creating your internal Life Coach

The power of self-talk has been shown, in research and by medical and communications professionals, to have psychophysiological outcomes[11]. The average person has 60 thousand thoughts a day! And most of that self-talk is about themselves, and mostly about negative arguments . . . *I shouldn't have done that . . . how can I be so stupid . . . . I will never be able to do this right . . . .*

Studies and reports supported by doctors and patients alike have shown that people can affect their health with their self-talk. If we understand the power of our minds and take an active role in deciding what to think, enhancing the positive messages we send to ourselves, we can face all of the challenges we bring on to ourselves just "by thinking about them". Thoughts affect our attitudes, our brain's neurotransmitters, and bodily functions such as breathing, sweating and body temperature. Most importantly, our thoughts affect our ability to face challenges.

Exercise:

1. Create a list of your self-critical statements that automatically come to mind when you do something that is new, challenging or when you didn't have a successful outcome in the past.
2. Create a "turn around argument" for that specific thought, concentrating on the argument for the opposite of that

---

[11]   Braiker, H.B. (1989). "The Power of Self-Talk." Psychology Today, December, pp. 23-27.

thought and the limitation that creates in your behaviors or actions.

3. Begin to take action with your "turn around" statement every time you become aware of the negative and self-critical statement. When you bring a negative statement to your awareness, then you can act on it. Otherwise negative statements are managing and directing your life without you even being aware of them!

Critical statement	Arguments	Turn Around Statement
Nobody likes me	Not even the president of the U.S. that does not know me?	Certainly there is people that likes me. May be I need to become more aware of them
I am not good at anything	*How did I make so far if I am not good at anything?*	I am good at something such as . . .
Everybody things I am not smart	Everybody? Even people that I have never seen?	I have some smart part of me since I can do X, X and X

I am never going to accomplish this goal	Never? How did I accomplish other goals then	I need to work harder and plan better to accomplish this goal

Assignment 19: Begin to appreciate yourself and others

Learning to appreciate your accomplishments and the accomplishments of others should be a day to day activity towards increasing your feelings of self-esteem and promoting self-esteem in others. You will never find anyone to complain about receiving a compliment or recognition. Have you?

You will have experienced feeling good when somebody gave you a compliment. Feeling good means that your level of Dopamine increased in your brain. Dopamine plays a major role in the brain system responsible for reward-driven learning. Every type of reward increases the level of dopamine transmission in the brain.

Making it a daily activity to reward yourself and complement others on a daily basis may allow you to keep your Dopamine levels at a healthy range or to increase it when you're feeling down.

Exercise:

While you are getting up in the morning, create your day, take ten minutes to create your personal appreciation list for that day, the day you are just about to begin.

Choose areas to appreciate, from skills and abilities that have allowed you to be who you are now, or identify the skills and abilities that you are about to call yours in an upcoming day.

Your appreciation list may sound include items such as:

- I appreciate my body; it takes me where I want to go and lets me live my life.
- I appreciate my mind. I use it without limitations whenever I chose to do it.
- I appreciate this day, which will allow me to test the best of me.

Think about whom you will appreciate that particular day, and what do you need to do to. You may need to use the phone, send an email or a letter, or make a personal visit.

As you incorporate your new behavior in your day to day regime, you will be creating a new habit, one of looking at your gifts and talents rather than your short falls and or limitations. Once you begin and get into the habit of doing it routinely, you will be in charge of creating your day, your week, your life.

Assignment 20: Begin to create the Life you want

Thoughts and ideas are unlimited. About sixty thousand today, with another sixty thousand tomorrow and for everyday for as long as you live. You cannot stop your thinking, not even when you go to sleep. Since you are going to have so many thoughts and ideas every day for the rest of your life, why don't you use this reality to begin to 'carve out' thoughts and ideas that will allow you to enjoy your life?

And, you know that negative thoughts make you feel sad and unhappy, while positive thoughts make you feel alive, happy and hopeful.

Creating thoughts and ideas on the mental plane by using words or pictures can be used to concentrate and direct your energy and strengthen the power of will. [12] Creating thoughts and ideas mentally are done through affirmations. Affirmations are positive statements which affirm or declare a desired objective as if it were already achieved. Attaching the objective to a visual image increases the power and strength of affirmations.

Having affirmations in several areas of your life allows you to override your self-defeating thoughts and restrict ideas running wild in your mind sixty thousand times a day! Affirmations will shift your perception, increase your motivation and allow you to take action to resolve the structural tension created by misalignment.

---

[12] David Spangler(1975) The Laws of Manifestation

Exercise:

Make a list of the things that you want to have, to do or to become. For example: *I want to have more patience, I want to be a good student, and I want to have a car.* Identify affirmations in different areas of your life, and write them in the present tense if you have already achieved them. Make them personal, short and specific, and state the feeling you will have if they were present in your life at this moment.

Some examples:

I want to have more patience.

I am enjoying my relationship with my family, by being loving, patient and caring every time we discuss issues.

I want to be a good student.

I am proud and excite, having excellent grades in all the subjects and enjoying my studies.

I want to have a car.

I am excited driving my four doors blue Honda, it is reliable and takes me wherever I want to go.

Assignment 21: Become Aware of your Thoughts and Emotions

Become aware that you are neither your thoughts nor your emotions. What you think to a large extent creates your emotions, as your thinking is responsible for the way you feel. The stories you create in your head will trigger some of the emotions you have chosen for that story.

When you say *"I am sad"*, that does not determine that **you** are sad, but that there are some thoughts or perceptions creating sadness in you. When you change the language of being sad, you are no longer part of the sadness and can begin to look at situations and thoughts that are sad without feeling sad.

Exercise:

To detach yourself from your thoughts and feelings, create a list of situations that you have encountered and identify the thoughts and emotions that were 'playing' in the background. Once you reflect on those, then you can bring the state of *Presence* in your life. It could be that you have brought forth those feelings and thoughts, if so then you can take action to change the situation, thoughts and feelings, or remove yourself from the situation. If there is nothing you carn do to improve the situation, then you can face and deal with it, calmly.

I am sad	I am thinking about a situation that created sadness in the past, and I am relieving the sadness.
I am angry	I am creating the feeling of anger because of a situation where I don't know how to respond, so far
I am nervous	I am making myself nervous by thinking that I do not have the skills for the interview tomorrow.
I am desperate	I am making myself desperate by being unable to find the skills I need to solve this situation

Facing reality is always an empowering process. Rather than 'being' your emotions and your thoughts, you need to become aware of them as an observer of your feelings and emotions. Becoming an observer will give you the ability to address just that, your thoughts and emotions, since you are neither your thoughts nor your emotions!

You are the 'being' behind the emotions and the thoughts, and you can look at the options and choose how you want to feel about them.

Assignment 22: Reclaiming your Personal Power

If you really think about it, you only have "this moment". When you are not living your life in the moment, you are either using your mind to bring about memories of feelings and situations from the past that you have chosen to use as *template* to evaluate the now, or you are thinking 'in the future', which is an experience that is not even here, yet you are anticipating outcomes.

You can be completely open to the future so as to either create whatever you want or resolve whatever may come, or you can bring templates from your past providing premature feelings and thoughts. How can you address the future without looking at your past? By becoming the observer again and choosing what you want to create in your future. It is not easy to create something from scratch, meaning without drawing on the past, but the opportunity to do so is always open.

Exercise:

Choose an area of your life for which you would like different outcomes than those that have occurred in the past. You may not want to repeat behaviors you have used in the past, given similar situations in the future, since those behaviors have not provided positive feelings.

When you think about a situation, visualize what past behaviors and emotions could come to cloud your new behaviors and feelings. Become aware of them as if the situations found in a movie, but do not again engage in them. Begin by analyzing and visualizing the experience you want to create in the future, one that is different from the past; this time you want a new experience and you want to feel different emotions. Remember that by behaving in a certain way in the past you have already created expectations in others. To change those expectations, you will likely need more than one opportunity to re-invent yourself and play out your new outcome!

Every time you want to create a new experience, remember the others are used to the "old you". So, to validate the 'new you', you have to be bigger than the time, bigger than the environment and the circumstances surrounding you.

Examples:

Situation	Habitual Behavior	New Behavior
Conversing with my son about his school work	Every time I get very emotional and upset, I begin to raise my voice and use hard discipline with him as to demonstrate who has the power.	I want to "understand" him and I will keep myself observing my responses to maintain calmness when speaking to him. I will become aware of to how to de-escalate when I lose my patient

Not being able to answer to my boss when I perceive him being critical of my work in a harsh full manner	When he approaches me in a critical manner I become silent and I don't know what to say. I get very critical of myself.	The next time he approaches me, I will be present in the conversation and look at his criticism in an open and constructive manner so I can be an active participant with his feedback

Summary

These twenty two assignments including the initial agreement are powerful tools. Do not underestimate their simplicity. If you choose to engage in taking full charge of your life the assignments will help you to move in the direction that you choose.

Once your understand the power of "self", anything that you want to experience in life, is literally one step away. Good luck!